"*Am I a Better Christ*ı parent, and it adds humor to some or the biggest questions that people of faith are facing within our culture. This book transcends the mundane and allows readers to follow along saying 'Oh I relate to this' on most pages. The brilliance of this book is that every page brings personal relatability and asks the questions that so many of us are afraid to confront. This book is healing, transformative, and aware of the human journey."

**Benjamin Higgins**, author of *Alone in Plain Sight* and president of Generous Coffee Company

"My whole life I've had questions. Questions I was afraid to ask because there would be ramifications. Maybe even ridicule. I was supposed to know the answer to these questions by now, after all. But sometimes it seems the pursuit of answers leads to even more questions. This book approaches difficult questions with honesty. Every reader will find at least one chapter that resonates. Mark Tabb's authenticity eventually leads readers to find hope and clarity despite any questions they may already possess."

**John Mark Yeats**, PhD, author and president of Corban University

# AM I A BETTER CHRISTIAN ON ZOLOFT?

And Other Questions About Faith
I Should Probably Keep to Myself

MARK TABB

R
Revell
*a division of Baker Publishing Group*
Grand Rapids, Michigan

Published by Revell
a division of Baker Publishing Group
Grand Rapids, Michigan
RevellBooks.com

Printed in the United States of America

Library of Congress Cataloging-in-Publication Data
Names: Tabb, Mark A., author.
Title: Am I a better Christian on Zoloft? : and other questions about faith I should probably keep to myself / Mark Tabb.
Description: Grand Rapids, Michigan : Revell, a division of Baker Publishing Group, [2025]
Identifiers: LCCN 2024041616 | ISBN 9780800746285 (paperback) | ISBN 9780800747169 (casebound) | ISBN 9781493450688 (ebook)
Subjects: LCSH: Christian life.
Classification: LCC BV4501.3 .T25 2025 | DDC 248.4—dc23/eng/20241122
LC record available at https://lccn.loc.gov/2024041616

Cover design by Derek Thornton, Notch Design.

The author is represented by the Ambassador Literary Agency.

Baker Publishing Group publications use paper produced from sustainable forestry practices and postconsumer waste whenever possible.

25  26  27  28  29  30  31       7  6  5  4  3  2  1

*For Valerie*

# CONTENTS

Introduction   9

**1.** Am I a Better Christian on Zoloft?   15

**2.** Can I Call Myself a Christian If I Don't Watch
   *The Chosen?*   29

**3.** Do I Really Have to Chase My Dreams?   43

**4.** Did Not Allowing My Children to Watch
   *The Simpsons* Make Any Difference?   57

**5.** Is God Sort of Mean?   69

**6.** If I Believe God Is in Control, Why Am I So Upset
   About the Last Election?   83

**7.** Why Don't I Feel It?   99

**8.** Did the Church in Ancient Ephesus Have a
   Creative Arts Director?   113

**9.** Can I Claim Jeremiah 29:11 as My Life Verse
   If I've Never Read the Book of Jeremiah?   125

**10.** What If I'm Wrong?   139

Afterword   153
Acknowledgments   157

# INTRODUCTION

I miss the days when I had all the answers. Today it seems I have nothing but questions. Long ago I knew everything. Now I wonder if I know anything. I miss the days of knowing everything, maybe because back then I still had 20/20 vision and a full head of hair. I miss having hair even more than I miss knowing everything. I often wonder why my hair fell out. They say you inherit your maternal grandfather's hair, which if that were true, I'd still need to go see a barber every couple of weeks. I don't know why my hair fell out except that maybe it has something to do with the fact that I have five daughters. Or maybe it's because I wore a ball cap through most of my childhood. Or maybe God made me bald in payback for my relentlessly mocking that one professor at my alma mater with the really, really, really bad comb-over. If so, everyone who attended my small college must be bald by now because you could not see this comb-over and not say something. They aren't, so maybe my being follicly challenged isn't divine retribution. Whatever made my hair fall out, I hope my grandsons don't inherit a head that creates its own halo in Zoom calls.

I don't just have questions about my long-lost once great society of hair. I have questions about just about everything. My questions aren't the profound, reality-bending variety my philosophy professor threw at me when I was a college freshman (although he did have a great head of hair for an old guy). I don't sit around wondering if all of reality is an illusion like life in the Matrix movies. Nor do I contemplate the possibility of alternate realities and parallel universes where another version of me still has a thick head of dark hair, which frees him to consider weightier issues like how to become a social influencer after the age of sixty. Instead I contemplate questions more grounded in reality, like am I a better Christian while taking the antidepressant Zoloft or can I really call myself a Christian if I have never watched a single episode of *The Chosen*.

I also wonder if it made any difference whatsoever that I didn't let my daughters watch *The Simpsons* when they were growing up or that instead of a Nintendo video game console, my daughters had a Socrates, which only had educational games. One of my girls became a doctor, so I think the answer to the last one is obvious. But she also identifies as an atheist who doesn't get cultural references, so maybe the jury is still out on the former.

I don't just have questions about the parenting decisions my wife and I sweated out during our child-raising years. I have lots of other questions concerning topics about which I was once more than certain. I have questions about God and life and myself and everything else I once had figured out. Some of these questions have been swirling around inside me for decades, like the question that first hit me long ago as I grew more and more distraught while watching election returns. That night I was on the verge of tossing a shoe at my television when suddenly the question hit me: If I believe God is in control, why am I so upset? I wish I could say that was the last time I allowed an election or one of life's unwanted surprises to upset me. Every time, I hear the same basic question rattling in my mind: *If God is in control, why am I so upset?*

Can I be completely honest? Sometimes I wonder about God's control. I wonder why he allows much of what happens in this world. Then I read some of what he did in the Bible, and I find myself wondering if he is really who my third-grade Sunday school teachers said he was and if he is really who I make him out to be. But then again, sometimes I wonder if I am who I make myself out to be. Are any of us? And yet the biggest question that I cannot escape is one that is pounding in my head right now: *What if I am wrong?*

That final question takes me right back to where we started: I miss the days when I had all the answers. Life is easy when you have all the answers. You don't have to think. You don't have to wrestle with life's plot twists and surprises. All you need to do is bounce along with all your prepackaged ideas and explanations for all of life. It's a dangerous way to live because you never learn, you never grow, you never expand your horizons, and thus you are not prepared for the day when your prepackaged ideas and explanations crash into the reality that is life. Life is actually doing us a favor when it refuses to fit the mold we try to stuff it into. It refuses to conform to easy answers because everything that makes life worth living is not easily explained. God is not. Relationships are not. Parenthood definitely is not. Neither is love or death or grief or anything else that makes life life.

Life feels simple when we have all the answers. The path grows much harder when all our answers get stripped down into the form of a question. Yet, I wouldn't have it any other way—as if I or anyone else has a choice. That is why I invite you to come along with me on this journey into a handful of the questions I find swirling around in my brain. I don't guarantee answers. Just the opposite. I didn't start writing this book to prop up everything about which I thought I was certain. Shakespeare once said that security is mortals' chiefest enemy.[1] I will go one step further than the Immortal Bard and say that certainty is the mortals' chiefest weakness. Certainty is when we already have all the answers. This book is an honest journey into the questions. Many have shaken me and opened the door to honest, thoughtful conversations with myself and with others, conversations that have deepened relationships while allowing me to grow. That's my goal for you in this book.

What follows may be divided into chapters, but that's a bit deceiving. Every chapter is a stand-alone essay built upon the title questions. Whether you read them in order or skip around to whichever catches your attention does not matter. The chapters do not build upon one another, although I highly recommend reading chapter 10 last.

Each chapter also includes a post-essay section addressed to specific readers. For example, at the end of the first chapter, "Am I a Better Christian on Zoloft?," I have a few words for those who, like me, have wrestled with depression and anxiety on some level. If this does not apply to you, feel free to skip. Think of the post-essay sections as a sort of post-credit scene in a superhero movie, except they do not set up the next chapter. Also, as in most superhero movies, I have inserted Easter eggs here and there, primarily for my daughters.

While you may prefer to read books as I do—that is, like the world may end if I don't get through it as quickly as possible— I wrote this book to be read at a leisurely pace. I recommend taking time after each essay to reflect upon the question asked. My goal is for each essay to be a conversation starter. That is

---

1. William Shakespeare, *The Tragedy of Macbeth*, act 3, scene 5, lines 32–33.

why this is a book of questions, not answers. Questions make for much deeper conversations, along with a more honest look within ourselves. As the final chapter makes clear, stepping outside our cocoons of certainty is not a bad thing. Instead, it opens us up to explore and to learn. We are never too old for either.

Finally, the essays that follow may all start with a question, but they are not all written the same. One reads like a testimonial while another sounds like I am speaking to a hostile crowd. One essay is a letter to my future self while another is a conversation between first the prophet Jeremiah and then the apostle Paul and an agent who has some helpful advice to aid them in marketing their work. I meant for each essay to be a bit humorous, although humor, like beauty, is definitely in the eye of the beholder.

## ONE

# Am I a Better Christian on Zoloft?

I guess I should go ahead and address the eight-hundred-pound gorilla in the room. Yes, I am on the antidepressant Zoloft. At least its generic form. Like a lot of us, I started taking it during the COVID pandemic. With time I was able to wean myself off of it, but eventually I realized I am easier to live with while taking it. Why am I sharing this with you, my dear reader? I have no idea. I will go ahead and report myself for a HIPAA violation, since this kind of personal information usually remains private. Too late for that. Even before I sat down at my keyboard to start writing this book, I told too many people the title for me to keep my secret. Yes, the title of this chapter and the book are based on my own personal experience. I really do wonder if I am a better Christian while taking Zoloft.

Now I will address the second eight-hundred-pound gorilla that just wandered into the room: What possible reason could I have for admitting such a fact? Honestly, I don't know. I should probably ask my doctor to prescribe something to keep me from talking so openly about topics many people keep to themselves.

Perhaps I could sidestep this problem by turning this book into a work of fiction starring a protagonist who just so happens to go through on-again, off-again battles with depression and anxiety. If anyone asked how much of that book was autobiographical, I could wave off the question and say, "These are just characters in a story. Any resemblance to any persons living or dead is purely coincidental."

But there is no coincidence. The truth is, this is my life. From time to time, I find myself in situations where my patience runs low and anxiety churns in my stomach and I feel a little like a volcano about to explode and all the while a little pinprick in the back of my mind keeps asking how differently I might handle the situation if I just had a little help from Pfizer.

This admission opens the door for a third eight-hundred-pound gorilla to crash this party (and we're definitely running out of room in here, so I hope this is the last one—but eight-hundred-pound gorillas have a mind of their own): Why do I need a little help from Pfizer in situations that test my patience and stir up anxiety? (And this question has nothing to do with how I found myself on an antidepressant in the first place. We will let that gorilla run free after I clear the room of the others.) As a person who has been quite vocal about following Jesus since grade school, albeit with a detour late in high school, and as a person with a theology degree and who served as a full-time pastor for a decade and a half and has also written several Christian books, shouldn't I overflow with patience? Shouldn't living out the admonition of Philippians 4:6, which tells me "do not be anxious about anything," be automatic by this point in my life? Of course! And most of the time it is, at least until I find myself in a situation that sneaks up on me and pushes just the right internal buttons to elicit a response that isn't as exactly Christlike. But these situations are rare.

Rare-ish.

Okay, in the interest of total transparency, perhaps these instances are not as rare as I want to believe. Now that I have started writing about them, I've suddenly become much more aware of them, the way you suddenly see a certain model of car everywhere even though you never noticed any on the road before you bought one. And that is where my latest moment of honesty took place, on the road, a couple of hours after my finished basement flooded, ruining the carpets and possibly the drywall. The full extent of the damage was yet to be determined.

I guess you could say I had a lot on my mind as I drove up our smallish town's primary north-south road, which for some inexplicable reason narrows to two lanes through downtown and past the hospital until it finally opens back up into a real road immediately prior to the intersection where I needed to turn left to buy some essentials to save the drywall in our finished but flooded basement. I headed north on this two-lane road with a thirty-mile-per-hour speed limit only to find myself stuck behind a driver that could not bring themself to push their car past twenty-five. At first I sighed. Then a green light I should have made easily turned red, which added another three minutes to my trip that felt like thirty. When the light finally turned from red to green, the driver decided, out of an abundance of caution, to drive even slower. "What on earth is your problem, buddy? Drive THE SPEED LIMIT!!!" I said quite loudly in my car even though I was alone.

No sooner were the words out of my mouth than my mind flashed to this chapter. *Where is the patience? Where is the kindness? Where is the self-control the Holy Spirit is supposed to bring to our lives according to Galatians 5?* Could I not have easily chosen all three rather than yell at a driver who could not hear a word I said?

I had no answer, only the realization that I handled this exact same situation much better when I was on Zoloft. Driving up State Street on an already very eventful Saturday, I had to wonder why I ever went off of it.

Now, before you start casting stones at me for my I-love-Jesus-but-I-yell-at-slow-drivers-when-I'm-in-a-hurry hypocrisy, let he who has never excused biting someone's head off first thing in the morning with the get-out-of-jail-free statement, "Well, I haven't had a cup of coffee yet this morning," cast the first stone. And let she who has never fallen onto her sofa after eight hours of dealing with an office full of stress inducers and said to no one in particular, "I need a glass of wine," throw another. Let those who have never become hangry and those who have never yelled at their internet service provider when they could not access their social media "news" feed cast the third and fourth. Let all those who have never leaned on caffeine or sugar or ice cream or Instagram likes or any other external source of peace and contentment stand in judgment of us all. But to the rest, which I think is most likely all of us, I have to ask: Shouldn't the inner working of God's Spirit be enough to get us through a morning when we don't have time to make it to the Starbucks drive-through? Shouldn't the power of God that is at work within us be stronger than a missed meal or two? (And yes, I know, the latter is the point of fasting, something else I've never been very good at.)

What is wrong with us that makes us need a little external help to be good Christians? For that matter, what does it even mean to be a good Christian? My search for an answer to that last question takes me back full circle to the question I keep trying to avoid: How did I discover I was a better Christian on Zoloft? To find that answer, I have to go back to why my doctor prescribed it for me in the first place.

## Back to the Beginning

I didn't know I was depressed when my depression first hit. I just didn't feel like myself. I might have even said, "I feel depressed," but I didn't mean depressed-depressed. I never thought about seeking professional help because I didn't have *that* kind of depression. No, what I felt inside was the natural response to situations beyond my control that had knocked my world off its blocks. I was down. Any normal human being would be.

But I stayed down.

That should have been my first clue that something bigger was going on. I didn't just feel down. I felt like a little invisible man had crept into my life and started beating me across the back with the flat side of a shovel. When I woke up in the morning, he was there. When I went to my office to start work, he was there. When I went to lunch, he was there. When I tried to enjoy some time with my wife and family, he was there beating me across the back with the flat side of a shovel day in and day out. He never stopped.

Instead of seeking help because, news flash, having a little invisible man hit you across the back with a shovel all day every day is not normal, I pressed on. *This too shall pass*, I told myself. Everyone goes through hard times, so why should I expect any different? Besides, I had good reasons to feel like I did. The very hard situation that had swallowed me up showed no signs of going anywhere. Of course I felt like I was being beaten across the back with the flat side of a shovel. That little man had a name, and that name was Life. It's what Life does. It beats you up. Get used to it!

Repeating that last sentence over and over was my first of many mistakes in dealing with depression. Mistake number two came after I lost my stepdad six years after losing my father. Rather than seek help, I chose to bury my grief under a load of work. I knew there was no way that work was going to make my grief go away, much less the little man with the shovel, but since when did something like facts ever get in the way of us doing what we want to do? I told myself that work gave me something else to fixate on, at least for a while.

And it worked, for a while. A short while. When it stopped, I made my third mistake in dealing with depression.

By this point I knew I had a real problem. My symptoms kept getting worse, not better. I even began to wonder if I was depressed-depressed and not just, you know, depressed. I now felt more than down. I discovered that somewhere along the way I had pretty much stopped caring about much of anything. Work had been my escape. Now I didn't care if I wrote another word. An agent brought me a really good story about a guy climbing Mount Everest. Normally I love that sort of thing. Instead, I told the agent, *No one cares. Hard pass.* I almost sought professional help, but then I noticed something that gave me hope that I could still pull myself out of this funk. The one time I felt really good, the one time I felt like myself, was on my road bike, riding long distances (at least long for me).

So that was mistake number three in dealing with depression. Rather than talk to my doctor or a therapist, I bought a new bike and rode a lot. I love riding my bike. When I'm on it, I feel like a little kid again. Problems, schmoblems. Go another five miles and you will feel right as rain.

Except I didn't. Not permanently. Exercise endorphins make you feel great, but they come with a steep crash after they wear off.

Exercise wasn't the answer, but I wasn't ready to throw in the towel and actually utter the words "I am depressed and I need help." Instead I tried all the little strategies that well-meaning people who have never gone through depression and anxiety suggest with their helpful advice, which is usually accompanied by Bible Band-Aids.

I counted my blessings. Didn't work.

I considered how other people faced much worse situations than me. Didn't work.

I prayed harder. Didn't work.

I went to church. Didn't work. A lot of Sundays I felt worse afterward.

I spent time with people I love. Didn't work.

I watched mindless comedies and baseball and so-ridiculous-they're-hilarious disaster movies to distract myself. Didn't work.

I tried reading, and I am a voracious reader. I'm writing this chapter on a Friday morning, and I've already read three books this week. Reading didn't work. Eventually I couldn't even pick up a book, much less read it.

And then one day I came to a point where I knew what I was experiencing was not a funk and it was not just a bad day. I also realized that the clock was now ticking on how much time I had to get help, which left me no choice. I called my doctor and made an appointment. For the first time I got completely honest with myself and with someone else, and I told him everything. That's when my doctor put me on Zoloft. The medication worked. The cloud lifted. Everyone lived happily ever after.

The end.

Except . . . of course there is more to the story.

## Better?

My cloud of depression and anxiety lifted, but since I live in Indiana and it was wintertime, the clouds in the sky remained all day every day for days and weeks at a time. My wife and I had all we could stand of the winter gloom and booked a trip to a sunny island for a romantic getaway. We hadn't traveled by plane in over a year because of the COVID shutdowns, which meant we were eager to get out of town. But of course, since this was post-COVID travel, once we arrived at the airport, we encountered what one all too frequently encounters at the airport: a situation with the ability to push just the right internal buttons to elicit a response that isn't exactly Christlike. I've been through enough airports and witnessed enough angry passengers to know that no one is immune from the occasional air-travel-crazies, including myself. Another romantic getaway several years earlier had been ruined by unnecessary delays that turned a quick getaway into an all-day slog. I didn't handle that situation particularly well.

Thankfully, on our post-COVID trip, we did not encounter anything to that degree. Even so, apparently my overall airport demeanor was different enough from my norm for my wife to turn to me at some point and smile and say something along the lines of, "I can really tell the difference your medication is making." I took this as the compliment she intended. But then I started thinking.

And thinking.

And thinking.

The more I thought about what my wife said, the more I realized that this antidepressant had done more than what was advertised. Not only had it lifted the cloud of depression that hung over me but the chemicals in my bloodstream made my outward behavior more calm, made me easier to be around. In a word, I acted more Christian than before. I could not help but admit, I was a better Christian on Zoloft.

Or was I?

In the interest of full disclosure, I have to admit that the title of both this chapter and this book started off as a bit of a joke that grew out of that trip. The first time I said the question out loud, I asked it within a group of friends more to get a laugh than anything else. I can happily report that since my friends are either easily entertained or too polite to embarrass me, they all laughed. Someone said something like, "Oh, you should write a book about that." I had already thought of that because since that day in the airport with my wife, I had not been able to get this question out of my mind. I may act more Christian, but am I really a better Christian on Zoloft?

Without a doubt I am more patient on Zoloft. Traffic delays roll off my back. I don't yell at other drivers. I find it much easier to stay calm in stressful situations, which was immediately put to the test a month after I started taking my medication. I prefer to keep the details to myself, but let it suffice to say that my wife and I have five adult daughters. With big families comes big drama, and we had all the drama we wanted and then some over the span of a week that felt like six months. Every morning when I took my little pill, I uttered the prayer, *Thank you, God, for putting me on this when you did.* So yeah, I have more patience on Zoloft.

Since patience and kindness go hand in hand, I must admit I am kinder while medicated. Most people I know, with the exception of a handful of jerks, exercise a basic level of kindness in most social situations. They may not go out of their way to do something nice for other people, but most people most of the time want to go along to get along. When exiting a parking garage after a concert or a ball game, most of us alternate letting cars into the line rather than jam our bumper up against the car in front of us. The vast majority of people exit a plane by rows, front to back, rather than run for the exit. However, when our patience is tested by a driver poking along at ten miles per hour under the speed limit and there's no way to get around him, basic kindness gives way to the law of the jungle. It's every person for themselves. I find jungle law kicks in far less often for me with an antidepressant/antianxiety drug in my system.

I could go down the list of other character qualities we usually associate with a good Christian and confess that, yes, Zoloft makes it easier to see those qualities in my life. Joy? Check. Peace? Check. Gentleness? Check. Fewer outbursts of anger? Check. Less worry? Check. More self-control? Check.

The answer to my title question thus seems obvious. From all outward appearances, I am a better Christian while taking Zoloft. However, outward appearances can be deceiving.

I may be a nicer guy while taking Zoloft, but that doesn't mean I am becoming more like Jesus as a result. Behavior modification is a side effect of the Christian life, not the point of it. I may putt along behind a driver doing eighteen in a thirty-five miles per hour zone without losing my cool, but the second great commandment[1] demands more. Loving my neighbor as myself means far more than ignoring behavior I normally find annoying. I can smile through traffic jams and airport delays and restaurants losing my order and all of life's other annoyances without loving anyone but myself. I don't have to lose my cool in order to be self-centered, which is the exact opposite of what it means to follow Jesus.

1. Matthew 22:39.

When I dig deeper into this question, I reach a point where I don't know that there are good Christians and bad Christians, just deeply flawed human beings trying to get in step with the Spirit. To be a Christian means to love God with everything that is in me because he loved me first. Some days I find my heart overflows with love and worship and adoration of the One who gave his son for me. Other days . . . we all have those other days. I may be patient with others. I may be the kindest person in the building. But that doesn't mean my heart is focused on God and loving him like he loves me. Medication can't make that happen, only a healthy combination of grace and faith.

And yet, I still find myself drawn to the question at the top of this chapter. My journey to the place where I finally admitted to my doctor that I needed help resonates deep in my spirit as something more than simply going on a medication to address symptoms I was experiencing. James 4:6 says that God opposes the proud but gives grace to the humble. I quote this verse to myself nearly every day. It, along with the great commandments to love God and to love my neighbor as myself, pretty much sums up what it means to be a follower of Jesus Christ. Zoloft the medication did not make me a better Christian, but the act of finally reaching the end of myself and confessing to my doctor that I was in a very bad place and I needed help was perhaps the most Christian thing I have ever done. I was broken. I was defeated. I was overwhelmed with despair. But rather than cling to my last shred of self-confidence, I uttered a simple sentence I had fought for longer than I care to admit: I need help.

God is opposed to the proud. But he gives grace to the humble. My finally admitting my inability to overcome my depression myself and asking for help was an act of complete and total humility on my part. More than that, this act opened me up to a fresh wave of the grace of God, and that, more than anything else, is what it means to be a Christian. I need grace. Lots and lots of grace. And whatever puts me in the position to receive it is something I will embrace, no matter how hard the road may be to find it.

## A Final Word for Those Who, Like Me, Have Struggled with Depression

I first uttered the title question as a bit of dark humor with a group of friends, some of whom have also struggled with anxiety and depression. We all laughed like sailors in a life raft making jokes about the sharks circling in the water. In other words, laughing feels better than crying when you need more of the former and less of the latter. I never cried through my depression, but when I opened up about it with people close to me, they did.

I write all this to say that I know how difficult it is to admit that you are struggling with depression. As you just read, I exhausted myself trying to convince myself that I did not have the big D depression. If I had been honest with myself sooner, I could have avoided much of the inner turmoil that ripped me up inside. I learned from my mistakes. About a year and a half after first going on medication for depression and anxiety, I weaned myself off. Not on my own. I did this under my doctor's watchful eye and with his full blessing. However, he made me promise that if my symptoms returned, I would not put off getting help as I had done the first time. About a year later I kept my promise. My doctor had since moved on, but I made the call anyways. If I stay on medication the rest of my life, I do not care. It helps, which means I will keep taking it.

Honesty is the first step to healing. If you are a follower of Jesus Christ, do not allow other people's bad theology to keep you from getting the help you need. Again, as you just read, I tried to pray my depression and anxiety away. In my mind I knew depression was nothing to be ashamed of. I also openly talked about how asking for help for mental ailments is no different than seeking help for more outwardly visible physical ailments. But I still had trouble admitting to myself that I needed help that went beyond prayer. I don't know why. Several years ago when I tore up my shoulder as a volunteer firefighter, I did not think twice about consulting an orthopedic surgeon. Do I believe God could have healed my shoulder? I don't just believe he could have, I believe he did. He simply used a doctor to do it. I prayed and prayed for God to lift my depression. He answered my prayers using a little pill I take first thing every morning.

Medication may not be the best treatment option for you. Only you and your doctor together can answer that question. There are other avenues available, including counseling. Again, there are those who claim that sincere Christ followers don't need such services and that prayer and the Bible should be enough. Those who say such things are fools. On more than one occasion I have sought out professional help from Christian counselors trained to deal with the situations I faced. They did not wave some magic wand and make all my troubles go away. But they helped. Even the act of opening up to someone can bring healing.

Whatever you do, do something. If you struggle with depression or anxiety or other mental health disorders, don't wait. Get help. You will be glad you did.

# TWO

# Can I Call Myself a Christian If I Don't Watch *The Chosen*?

A friend at church started talking about a streaming series that depicts the life of Christ. My friend talked like he assumed I was watching it as well. When I told him I was not, he said something along the lines of I have to check it out because I will love it. Then the conversation took a turn. I told him I had seen part of it, and it wasn't really for me. He looked at me like I had just said I don't like chocolate chip cookies or pizza. Who in their right mind doesn't like chocolate chip cookies or pizza!? And what kind of Christian doesn't watch a show about Jesus!? The conversation was not an isolated event. I get the same reaction from people who assume I fill my life with other aspects of the Christian subculture, from faith-based movies and television shows and podcasts and television and radio preachers to Scripture-filled home decor and nonstop worship music, along with sending my kids to faith-based schools or homeschooling them. I've had so many of these conversations that I thought it best to simply set the record straight with an imaginary come-to-Jesus meeting with those immersed in the Christian subculture to clear things up once and for all. You will only hear my side of the meeting, but I will do my best to repeat the questions thrown at me.

Thank you all for being here today. I know many of us have had at least partial conversations about several of the points I plan to touch on today, which is why I wanted to take this opportunity to set the record straight. So, here we go. I might as well get the big question out of the way first. No, I don't watch *The Chosen*. I hear that gasp in the back. What's that, you ask? Have I even tried it? Yes, I have. And no, I still don't watch it. Excuse me, please, the gentleman in the back. Yes, you. Would you please check on that woman right over there? She seems to have fainted.

As I was saying, I don't watch *The Chosen* and . . . What did you ask? Christian?

Yes, I consider myself a Christian. Yes, I know *The Chosen* is about Jesus. Yes, I am aware it is the same Jesus. At least it is supposed to be. Excuse me? What did I mean by that last remark? Only that the show is the writers', directors', and actors' interpretation of the life of Christ. I'd say the actor who plays Jesus captures the character of Jesus as much as, I don't know, Jon Voight did as Franklin Roosevelt in *Pearl Harbor*. Yes, that Jon Voight. Yes, I believe he was in *Anaconda*. No, I don't think *Anaconda* was based on a true story.

If there are no other questions, then, as I was saying, I don't watch *The Chosen* for the same reason . . . What's that? Yes, the rumors are true. Sixteen years full time and, I don't know, another seventeen or eighteen part time. Yes, pastor. P-A-S-T-O-R. Yes, I went to school for it. Theology and Greek and Hebrew and church history, yes, I studied them all. Yes, I am ordained and everything. What kind of church hires someone who doesn't watch shows about Jesus? I'm not sure I understand your question.

Wait. Hold on. Sir. Yes, you there walking in the door. We do not allow torches or pitchforks in this room. Please take them outside. The protest signs as well. What's that? You'll be waiting for me when I leave? Okay, that's good to know. There's also a crowd gathering. Why, exactly? They're also waiting for me. Okaaaay. Again, why exactly? Oh. I guess I *will* see.

All right, I think I've said enough about *The Chosen* for one lifetime. What's that, you ask? Do I watch other faith-based movies and shows? I don't see what that . . . If I don't support those making Christian movies and shows then I am supporting the garbage coming out of the out-of-touch, leftist, communist Hollywood, you say. What does one have to do with . . .

Radio? I'm not sure anyone actually listens to the radio these days. Oh, streaming radio like iHeart. Yes. Oh, wait. Christian radio? Do I stream Christian radio? Not usually, although I still very much enjoy Christian rock bands like Audio Adrenaline and Relient K. And Switchfoot has been one of my favorite bands since I first heard "Chem 6A" thirty years ago. Love their music.

Wait. You don't mean music but preaching. Do I listen to sermons online or over the radio? No. Why? It's just not something that particularly appeals to me. If I do listen to talk radio or podcasts, which isn't that often, I usually listen to something about baseball. Is that not a good enough answer? It's not. Okay.

*Where did my kids go to school?* someone just shouted from the left side over there. You mean, college? I'm not sure what that has to do with anything, but if you must know, my oldest daughter went to a small private school in Illinois and my . . .

Wait. Not college? Grad school? Okay one went to med school in Indiana and another is . . .

Oh. Not grad school but *grade* school. You want to know where my children went to grade school? You realize that my oldest daughter started kindergarten in 1990? What? Doesn't matter? Okay. For what it's worth, all five of my children went to public schools and graduated from the same public high school in the small Indiana town where we lived forever.

Uh, I'm not sure I understand that question. How could I do what to them? To the schools? I mean, my daughters were excellent students. They weren't troublemakers like I was back in the 1970s . . . Oh, not the schools but my daughters. Did I not love my kids enough to shield them from those godless public school teachers and send them to a Christian school or homeschool them? What makes you think the teachers were godless? My oldest sister and her husband are both retired schoolteachers and they both love Jesus. What? Doesn't matter? All public school teachers are the devil, you say. Uh, does your last name happen to be Boucher?[1] No, no reason.

*Why am I doing this to myself?* I think someone just called out. Doing what, exactly? Exposing myself as a what? A *radical*? A *liberal*? Are you sure you don't want to throw in fanatical and criminal? *What's that supposed to mean?* you ask. I guess you didn't listen to the same bands I did growing up in the seventies.

All right, all right, this is getting out of hand. I need everyone to stop shouting at me for a couple of minutes. I am not here to argue with anyone, but if you would please find your seats for

1. This reference is for my daughters.

just a moment, I would like to ask you a few questions of my own. What? Yes, you are free to leave if you must, but I encourage you to stay because I really want your honest answers to my questions. No, I'm not trying to trick you into saying something ridiculous that will end up on YouTube. I won't even record your answers, just my questions. In fact, you don't even have to voice your answers, but I do ask that you seriously consider the questions. No, I can't make you do anything. Thank you for pointing that out.

Any other disruptions before we continue? Yes, man with the pitchfork. You're still waiting outside for me after this is over. That's good to know.

Actually, I'm glad you came back inside, pitchfork man, and thank you for at least leaving your torch outdoors. You seem to be very concerned about my choices in entertainment, as though those have any bearing on the faith I profess. Oh but it does, you say? And why is that exactly? May I quote you? Thank you. The man with the pitchfork tells me that my choices in entertainment are an accurate window into my relationship with God because, according to Romans 12:2, we are not to "conform to the pattern of this world, but be transformed by the renewing of your mind."[2] Therefore, if I watch the same movies as everyone else and listen to the same music as everyone else and send my kids to the same schools as everyone else and read the same books as everyone else and basically live like everyone else, I am conforming to the pattern of this world, like everyone else. That is why all serious believers should support moviemakers who produce films and series that have a strong Christian message and that avoid the usual bad language and violence and sexual content, real or implied, that Hollywood

2. NIV.

fills everything with. I believe the word the man in the audience used was *wholesome*. We should support wholesome entertainment, as all serious Christians do.

The same goes for music, you say. Instead of secular music with its secular messaging, being transformed means filling our lives with music that is positive and, dare I say, encouraging. Nothing fills that bill better than worship music. One of God's purposes for every human being is worship, and therefore we should fill our lives with worship music. Not only does it fulfill God's purpose but it is also safe. My kids can listen to it, and I don't have to worry about what they are hearing. Is this an accurate summation of what you just shouted? Great.

What's that, you say? Someone just pointed out that my favorite band doesn't advertise itself as a Christian band anymore. In fact, they often appear in shows with secular bands. They asked how Christian a band could be if they played in the same shows as secular bands and did not stop in the middle of their concerts to either include an altar call or at least give a clear presentation of the gospel. Real Christian bands always do both, along with giving the audience an opportunity to give toward the band's favorite Christian outreach charity. You just expect that when you go to a concert.

I'm glad you used that word, *expect*, because really, what all of this comes down to is what others expect of someone who claims to be a follower of Jesus Christ. Okay, okay, okay. I hear you loud and clear. You are not legalists. You have nothing in common with the old-school, hard-shell types who say women must wear dresses at all times and never cut their hair and men cannot have hair that touches either their ears or their collars. You are not saying all real Christians read only the King James Bible. Yes, I noticed you quoted the NIV earlier, sir. Good for you. Nor are you saying that somehow following a bunch of rules makes you more worthy of God's grace. Yes, grace is free. I agree.

But, correct me if I'm wrong, what you *are* saying is that not conforming to the pattern of this world means separating ourselves from most—yes, I know it is impossible to say all—of the bad stuff the world produces and instead surrounding ourselves with those things that remind us of the things of God. Oh. Yes. And with things that are safe in order to protect both our own minds and especially the tender minds of our children and grandchildren. You just expect a serious Christ follower to conform to this standard, correct?

Why did I use the word *conform*? Because that's what it is. Although it's unspoken, when you go to church or hang out with other Christians, you feel a certain pressure to like certain "Christian" things and agree with certain viewpoints and basically conform to the image of what a good Christian does. Now, let's be honest. Most Christians don't conform to these expectations. We can talk all day about how much we love a series like *The Chosen*, but in the privacy of our own homes, we also watch whatever is trending on Netflix. That's why these shows are trending. It's not just the secular world watching. But the pressure to conform keeps us from admitting we watch these shows or listen to certain types of music. Instead we watch and feel guilty about it. For some, the more guilty they feel about their own guilty pleasures, the more outspoken they are against them and the more judgmental against those who also indulge. Our anger with ourselves comes out in railing against godless Hollywood and how horrible the trash they put out today is, unlike what they put out a generation ago.

The only problem with that argument is that when you go back and watch, say, old John Wayne movies, swearing may be minimal, but that doesn't make the films any less cringeworthy with the way women are treated, to say nothing of racial attitudes. Don't believe me? Check out *McLintock*. The movie may not have any sex or nudity or graphic violence, but sexism oozes from its pores. Good grief, the movie poster shows John Wayne putting Maureen O'Hara over his knee and spanking her publicly! What's worse is the fact that this was treated as high comedy.[3] And then there is the way in which the portrayal of Native Americans reinforces every stereotype prevalent in 1963. Yeah, I don't think we can point to movies of the past as paragons of virtue.

With that little journey into the past out of the way, would you mind me going back to talking about conformity? Not conforming to the pattern of the world does not mean choosing conformity to the pattern of another subculture. Now listen, before you light up the torches again, and yes, I can see them hidden under your seats, I am not dissing any Christian radio stations or the latest Christian movies. If you love them, good for you. Watch them. Enjoy them. Invite your friends to see them as well. And if you do not want your child to attend the local public school and instead want to send them to a Christian school or to homeschool, you have to do what you think is right.

But don't look down on another Christ follower who makes different choices. The apostle Paul wrote in Romans 14:1–4:

Accept other believers who are weak in faith, and don't argue with them about what they think is right or wrong. For instance,

---

3. *I Love Lucy* regularly featured Ricky turning Lucy over his knee like she was a naughty three-year-old.

one person believes it's all right to eat anything. But another believer with a sensitive conscience will eat only vegetables. Those who feel free to eat anything must not look down on those who don't. And those who don't eat certain foods must not condemn those who do, for God has accepted them. Who are you to condemn someone else's servants? Their own master will judge whether they stand or fall. And with the Lord's help, they will stand and receive his approval.

"Don't argue with them about what they think is right or wrong." That's a verse I think we would all do well to memorize. Don't argue with others who confess to love Jesus but who do not conform to your expectations, or vice versa. What you watch, what you listen to, how you vote, what you choose to eat and drink, all these decisions must be based upon your own convictions, not those of others.

The problem of expectations was just as volatile in the first century. Romans 14 is not the only instance where Paul addresses it in his letters to the churches. In Colossians 2:16–17 he writes, "So don't let anyone condemn you for what you eat or drink, or for not celebrating certain holy days or new moon ceremonies or Sabbaths. For these rules are only shadows of the reality yet to come. And Christ himself is that reality." Christ is the reality, not all the expectations we feel we must live up to. And honestly, isn't most of this pressure self-inflicted? If I didn't know better, I'd say the guy with the pitchfork just nodded in agreement with me.

There's an even greater problem with confusing activities like watching certain shows and listening to certain music or watching certain news outlets with living a transformed life. It's not our activities Romans 12:2 says need to be transformed but our minds. God wants to transform us into new people by changing the way we think. Not *what* we think but the *way* in which we think. The difference is huge. When I allow the pressure of expectations or the opinions of others to shape the way in which I live, my mind does not have to be engaged. I just have to follow along. You say playing cards is bad but dominoes are good? Okay. Dominoes it is. Dancing is bad, you say, but roller skating is good, then let's skate away. Yes, I did grow up Baptist. How could you tell? What makes dominoes more holy than cards? I have no idea. I don't think anyone down at the Baptist home office can tell me either. I once heard it had something to do with gambling, as if you can't gamble on dominoes. Or maybe it had to do with fortune-telling, but you don't need cards for that. Just a palm.

And that's the problem. A mind in neutral, pulled along by cultural forces either "sacred" or "secular," is not a transformed mind.

But shouldn't we only consume Christian media and participate in Christian activities anyway, since they are safe? The answer to this question is a huge NO if you do it with your mind disengaged. How do you know any song from a "Christian" artist is safe? Well, it doesn't talk about sex or drugs like rock and roll always does. The singer is singing about God, for crying out loud. But that doesn't mean the ideas about God in the song are biblical. One popular worship song includes a line about how Jesus didn't want heaven without us. Sounds great. Where exactly might this be found in the Bible? Another talks about speaking the word "Jesus" over my anxiety and depression and over my family, basically over everything about which I have a concern. Again, this sounds great, but . . . once again, where exactly do we find this in the Bible? Maybe I'm nitpicking, but to me, this song reduces Jesus to a sort of magic word that makes all our problems disappear. But that's not what the song is saying, you might protest. Then what is it saying? We should all ask ourselves that question with any song, Christian or secular, and any movie and TV series and book and whatever it may be. And we can only ask such questions with a mind that is fully engaged.

Even the most innocuous, vanilla, non-offensive forms of entertainment are not necessarily safe. I watched part of a faith-based movie the other night. I couldn't make it to the end because the form of Christianity it presented was not the faith of the Bible. Sure, they talked about believing in Jesus, as expected. However, faith came across as nothing more than positive thinking and reciting worn-out clichés. My wife audibly groaned when one of the main characters actually said, with all seriousness, "Well, you know, when God closes a door, he opens a window." I don't think that's what Paul said when he had to go out a window in Damascus to keep from being put to death by the angry mob that was waiting just outside the door for him. Yes, this movie was unbelievably safe, as though the producers went out of their way to present the rosiest version of Christianity they could possibly come up with. Unfortunately, it was not honest. It felt like some rough, gruff redneck changing out of his dirty jeans and Lynyrd Skynyrd T-shirt with the sleeves cut out, washing the back of his neck and scraping the three-day growth off his chin, then changing into a pair of chinos and a buttoned-down collared shirt to try to impress a girl on their first date. Eventually the "Sweet Home Alabama" is going to come rushing out of him. It always does.

This movie was not alone in the idealized, happily-ever-after presentation of the Christian life. The faith presented in many shows and in music and novels is one where everything works out in the end, where problems all go away, and the good guys always win. You don't find that in the Bible. I know, I know, I know. When Jesus returns, we will see God's ultimate victory. But that doesn't mean this is the real-world experience of most Christ followers. Starting with Abel in the book of Genesis, the good guys didn't just finish last. Many of them ended up dead. When we pretend otherwise, when we surround ourselves with "Christian" media that tries to tell us that God is going to give us a wonderful life where our troubles will be few and our blessings will overflow, we set ourselves up for huge disappointment. Or worse. We will lose faith and blame God when our expectations for what he is supposed to do never materialize.

Whew. Sorry. I got a little carried away there. Uh, well, there's a good reason for that. I was once firmly in your shoes. Yeah, I probably would have helped light all your torches a couple of decades ago. I have some experience in this area, because one of the first things I did when I got serious about Jesus was to burn all my rock albums in my parents' burn barrel. It's a long story that begins with my spinning a Led Zeppelin album backward. Years later, my oldest daughter recently reminded me, when she asked for a Mariah Carey CD, my wife and I gave her Rebecca St. James instead. St. James was a popular Christian artist back in the 1990s and early 2000s, a safe alternative to someone like Mariah Carey, we thought. I also walked out of many an offensive (to me) movie, and I didn't have a lot of patience with those who did not share my zeal.

So what happened? Grace. Lots and lots of grace from God, patience from my family, and slowly having my eyes opened to the real meaning of not conforming to the pattern of this world.

All of this takes us back to Romans 12:2, the verse about nonconformity. In the original language in which this passage was written, it literally says, "Do not conform to this age." Age. Not world. Most Bible translations include this in a footnote. So what's the difference, you may ask. Everything. Not conforming means more than rejecting the actions and activities of a world that rejects Jesus. Not conforming to this age and instead having our minds transformed by God means rejecting the spirit of this age, its defining characteristics. And what is this day and age's defining characteristic? Division. Hate. Intolerance of any conflicting opinions or outlooks. That's what we must guard ourselves against, and the only way to do it is through a transformed mind. This is true nonconformity.

## A Final Word of Encouragement to Fellow Misfits

If you do not feel like you fit in, join the party. Neither do I. Neither do a lot of people who follow Jesus. We don't fit in with the old crowd with which we once ran, and we don't exactly fit in with every Christian we might run into at church. The good news is you don't have to. Diversity of opinions and viewpoints is a good thing. If everyone thinks the same way and acts the same way and votes the same way and watches the exact same shows and listens to the exact same music and reads the exact same books and basically clones themselves to all the others in the group, you don't have unity but uniformity. The difference is striking. Unity comes when we don't see eye to eye but choose to love each other and work together in spite of our differences. Diversity makes us stronger. Seeing everything through the same lens as everyone else leaves us open to huge blind spots. If we are all looking east, we never see the danger approaching from the west.

So hang in there, misfits. Choose to love where you don't fit in. Those who see the world completely different than you will also help spot problems approaching in your blind spots just as you will for them. Loving people who think like us and act like us and look like us is easy. God creates diversity to teach us what love really is.

So please don't hate me for not watching *The Chosen*.

## THREE

# Do I Really Have to Chase My Dreams?

The best life is the dream life. Dream job. Dream house. Dream spouse. You plan a dream wedding then take off on a dream honeymoon. You start a dream family and load them into your dream car as you drive away on dream vacations. The kids grow up and pursue their dream futures and attend their dream schools with their dream majors before moving on to their own dream jobs and dream houses and dream spouses. Once the kids have moved out, you start planning the dream retirement with dream trips to dream locations. Not even a dream life lasts forever, so you think about that dream departure with the dream kids with their dream families gathered around you, but not until you've lived eighty, ninety, or one hundred years. A long life, that's the dream. Before you leave your dream life, you plan your dream funeral and give instructions for the dream spot where you want your remains buried or ashes scattered. Once you ultimately move to the great beyond, you plan to live the final dream in the dream heaven you've always dreamed about. Life is all about chasing the dream.

Isn't it?

But what if I actually enjoy my ordinary job and am perfectly happy with a very ordinary house? Does that mean something is wrong with me? Am I just as married with an ordinary wedding, and what if I can only afford an ordinary honeymoon? An SUV or minivan with a third row of seats may be boringly ordinary, but it sure comes in handy since children's car seats and boosters won't fit in the dream car. What if I don't mind non-Instagrammable vacations in a local state park because at least we were able to get away as a family for a few days? If student loan payments and replacing HVAC systems pushed saving for that dream retirement back until I know that spending winter months on an exotic beach is never going to happen and instead most of the dream trips will consist of going to see the grandchildren, does this mean I am doomed to unhappy golden years?

I guess what I'm asking is do I really have to chase my dreams? Even questioning dream chasing feels a little unorthodox. Or is heretical a better word? The opposite of dream chasing is of course settling, and settling is a curse word when all the voices around us tell us to aim higher and dream bigger and pursue our passions. No one can stop you but you, we're told, so does that make it wrong to stop and say good enough is good enough? It certainly feels wrong.

Do your best, we're told. Be all that you can be. Maximize your potential. Go for the gold. And of course, change the world. You can, you know, because you are special. But what if I don't feel so special and I don't think the world wants to be changed, and instead of maximizing my potential, I'd really rather go outside and play catch with my grandson?

## Confessions of a Habitual Dream Chaser

I have to be honest with you, dear reader. I can't believe I'm actually writing this chapter. For most of my life I've been a dream chaser, a risk taker, an I-want-to-live-without-regrets kind of guy. I've changed careers more than once and moved my family cross-country not once but twice, all because I felt a divine calling to do so. I called my first book *Uncommon Adventures* because that's always been my approach to life. Make goals. Dream dreams. And then work hard to make them happen. Once one dream is caught, look for the next one on the horizon.

Now, I'm not so sure about my dream-chasing lifestyle. I don't know when doubt started creeping in. I didn't notice it until I was sitting in church one Sunday listening to a friend preach on this very topic. He cited a couple of Bible passages to explain how God created us to do great things, wonderful things, world-changing things that defy our wildest expectations. He then challenged the audience to let our imaginations take flight, to dream, if you will, about all the wonderful things God might have waiting for us in our futures.

The dream chaser in me should have shouted an amen or two, or at least nodded along in agreement. But instead of feeling inspired, all I could think was, *Really?* in a tone that told me I had already changed my mind about what I'd always believed. When *Really?* flashed in my brain, I was more than a little shocked. No. Shocked isn't the right word. I actually felt like a seven-year-old who discovers his parents stuffing his stocking with gifts on Christmas Eve. I didn't want to see what I had just seen, but I also knew I should have figured this out a long time ago.

One of my historical heroes, William Carey, the father of the modern missions movement, famously said in 1792 that we are to expect great things from God and attempt great things for God.[1] You can only imagine how my dream-chasing, risk-taking, live-without-regrets brain latched on to those words when I first read them in college. These words shaped how I read parts of the Bible and how I came to see my dream chasing as a divine mandate, in particular Ephesians 2:10 and 3:20–21. The former says, "For we are God's masterpiece. He has created us anew in Christ Jesus, so we can do the good things he planned for us long ago," while the latter says, "Now to him who is able to do immeasurably more than all we ask or imagine, according to his power that is at work within us, to him be glory in the church and in Christ Jesus throughout all generations, for ever and ever! Amen."[2] When I read these verses through the lens of "expect great things from God and attempt great things for God," they became a divine mandate to dream bigger, aim higher, and chase harder. The former tells me that God created me to do great things, and the latter tells me that since God is the one at work within me, these great things will defy the imagination. And I can imagine a lot!

However, the apostle Paul isn't telling his audience to dream bigger but to go about their everyday life in a different way. Instead of following our basest appetites like we did when we thought our lives were only about us and what we wanted,[3] God has a new path for us to walk, a life of doing good things he's planned out.[4] As I read these verses in that light, I can't help but think of one of my favorite lines from the old Disney cartoon *Robin Hood*, when the Sheriff of Nottingham says,

1. J. W. Morris, "Narrative of the First Establishment of This Society," *Periodical Accounts Relative to the Baptist Missionary Society*, vol. 1 (J.W. Morris, 1800), 3.
2. NIV.
3. Ephesians 2:1–3.
4. Ephesians 2:10.

"There goes Friar Tuck, the old do-gooder out doing good again." That's pretty much the idea. Follow Jesus and you'll end up doing good stuff instead of bad, living an unselfish life rather than a selfish one. The people who first read his letter didn't read more into it because dream chasing wasn't exactly an option. Most were illiterate and many were slaves. Visions of greatness didn't fill their heads when they heard Paul's words. Why would it ours?

In fact, the whole idea of refusing to accept the sky as the limit when there are footprints on the moon is glaringly missing from both the Old and New Testaments. In a later letter, Paul wrote the church in the Greek city of Thessalonica to "make it your goal to live a quiet life, minding your own business and working with your hands, just as we instructed you before. Then people who are not believers will respect the way you live, and you will not need to depend on others."[5] I may be wrong, but minding your own business and living a quiet life sound a little like, oh, what's the word I'm looking for, *settling* for a rather ordinary life. Rather than encourage believers to go out and attempt great things, world-changing things, the things of dreams, things that will make a difference for God, Paul went on to tell the church in ancient Corinth, "Whatever you do, do it all for the glory of God."[6] Whatever you do, not great things per se but basically anything, big, small, or in between. The *what* matters far less than the *why*.

So what does all this mean? In a word, it means you can relax, stop worrying about trying to accomplish something great with your life, and instead just live it. God's not sitting in heaven tapping his fingers, waiting for you to go out and do something

5. 1 Thessalonians 4:11–12.
6. 1 Corinthians 10:31.

amazing that will cure all the world's problems. Instead, God calls you and me to love him and love people wherever we happen to be and whatever we happen to be doing. That's the beauty of God's grace. It gives meaning to the ordinary even if we cannot quantify it in terms of some greater purpose. There doesn't have to be a greater purpose. The good works God planned in advance don't even have to look like something even remotely religious. I'll probably have to turn in my ordination papers for this one, if I can even remember where they are, but we don't even have to go out and volunteer at our local church or nonprofit. If you want to, great! But you don't have to in order to live an extraordinarily ordinary life that glorifies God, no dreams required.

I had this truth driven home to me recently at a funeral, of all places. I'd known Patrick for many years, although I did not know him well. All that changed at his funeral. Patrick lived alone in an apartment in a small town. He did not own a car. He did not have an important job. His life did not check off a single box on any high achiever's bucket list. Yet, at his funeral one person after another stood and talked about the impact Patrick had on their lives through his kindness and joy. Over the course of the twenty-two years he lived in this small town, he got to know nearly everyone who lived there, even though most could not communicate with him unless they went out of their way to learn sign language. But his deafness didn't stop Patrick from getting to know people as he volunteered around town and at his church. He was a fixture at all the local sports and charity events. Even more so, he was a fixture in town, where he always had a smile for everyone he met as he walked everywhere he went. Now the streets seem much emptier, colder.

Patrick lived a remarkable life even though he never did anything earth shattering or world changing. He simply lived an ordinary life while loving God and loving people in his own way. And that was enough.

It was exactly enough.

## I'm Not Giving Up That Easily!

I have never in my life spent as much time trying to write a single chapter as I have with the one you are now reading. Altogether, with all the brainstorming and outlining and starts and stops with different versions spread out over the past six months— yes, months—I have written enough words for this one chapter to fill at least half of this entire book. Probably more. In other words, writing this chapter has been harder than I expected. The heading of this section tells you why.

I do not want to give up chasing my dreams so easily. I find it very difficult to turn loose of the idea that a life best lived revolves around purpose and meaning and mattering, with goals to set and dreams to chase and catch. Every January my wife asks me what big plans I plan to pursue this year, because I always have BIG plans. Or at least I did up until a year or two ago. These days, not so much. And I don't like it. What I know in my head and what I believe in my heart are locked in a life-or-death battle. The dream chaser in me refuses to tap out.

Now, before I continue, I do need to make one huge clarification. If you are a goal setter and a dream chaser and see yourself as someone who senses a higher calling on your life, God bless you. If it works, keep doing what you are doing. I am not saying that setting goals and chasing dreams is in any way wrong. Thirty years ago, I had the crazy dream that I could write for a living. It took a decade of chasing, but I finally got there. The fact that my wife has a really good job helped. Be that as it may, I have zero regrets about pursuing my passion for writing as a vocation. Yes, writing to me feels like a divine calling, and even the process of wrestling with the keyboard to produce words is, for me, an act of worship. I love my job more than I can put into words. (And I'm a wordsmith.) The whole point of this chapter is to give us all a little grace and reassure us that we don't *have* to chase our dreams, but if you want to, more power to you. I hope you catch a few.

Having said all of this, and after taking a long look at myself in the mirror, I think it only right to encourage every dream chaser out there to stop for just a moment and ask a question we're usually too busy chasing dreams to ask ourselves: Why? That is, why do you feel compelled to chase your dreams? Why do you feel restless deep down inside when life feels like it is just plodding along? What makes you feel like you are made for more? What makes the idea of settling feel so wrong? I guess what I am really asking is what is it you really want when you are out chasing your dreams?

Be warned. If you are a hardcore dream chaser, you may not want to keep reading, because asking myself these questions is what started my journey of self-discovery that became this chapter.

## Is It Worth It?

I didn't just wake up one day and start asking myself these questions. No, I made the mistake of deciding to spend a month or so reading and rereading and meditating upon one of my favorite books of the Bible, the book of Ecclesiastes. The book might as well be called "Confessions of a Dream Chaser," because that's what it is. The writer was the classic overachiever.

He was a king, after all. And a writer. And a builder. You discover in his words a restlessness, a drive to accomplish more and more and more. The book of Ecclesiastes is basically him stepping back from all he has done and asking himself, What have I really accomplished? And here's his answer: Nothing. It's all empty, he concludes, like chasing after the wind. Anyone else would look at what he has done and tell him he's nuts to question the value of his accomplishments. Get the guy some Zoloft, some might even say. However, when you read Ecclesiastes, you understand the writer is absolutely right. Here's why.

No matter what you accomplish in this life, it won't last. You can accumulate great wealth, but in the end you will die and someone else will spend it. If the accumulation of wealth or honors is your why behind your dream chasing, you will end up frustrated, no matter how many of your goals you reach.

You can build great buildings and plant orchards and leave your mark on this world, but the memory of you will quickly fade away. And not just after you die. Even in the ancient world, people's time in the spotlight was brief. Again, if renown is what you seek, you may get it, but it won't last. Then what are you left with?

Worst yet, one of the most common sights of all is the person who works hard, builds what looks like a great life, but for whatever reason they can never truly enjoy it. That restlessness inside won't let them, because they are so focused on the next dream to catch. This is the warning that hit closest to home for me.

On top of everything else, the writer of Ecclesiastes points out that most people who are driven to do more, who aim higher, and who refuse to be satisfied with the ordinary are motivated by plain old envy.[7] That's a drive that can never be

7. Ecclesiastes 4:4.

satisfied because no matter how many dreams you catch, there's always someone out there who has caught more.

As I sat and contemplated all of this, I was struck by another thought. I went back to all the "Christian" motivational talks I've both delivered and heard, all the times I've used passages like Ephesians 2:10 to rally the troops, like Knute Rockne telling the boys to go out there and win one for the Gipper. The original title for this chapter was "Are We Really Destined for Greatness?" because that's the message I have heard and delivered within the Christian subculture most of my adult life. We are destined to do great things. Wonderful things. World-changing things. Yet that's not what the Bible says. So why do I need it to say that it does? Perhaps the only way to get myself and others motivated is to make my restlessness some sort of divine calling. The plain old ordinary doesn't exactly motivate us to jump up and down with excitement or storm the gates of hell. Instead, it leaves us with more of a "meh" response. At least it does me. I need to attempt great things and expect great things because ordinary things do not get my blood pumping, even though the ordinary is where even the most dedicated dream chaser spends the vast majority of their life.

### The Real Dream

The writer of Ecclesiastes hits his pinnacle of depressing thoughts for dream chasers near the end of the fifth chapter. He writes:

> People leave this world no better off than when they came. All their hard work is for nothing—like working for the wind. Throughout their lives, they live under a cloud—frustrated, discouraged, and angry.[8]

8. Ecclesiastes 5:16–17.

52

However, he offers hope in the next three verses, which are, incidentally, the real genesis for the chapter you are reading:

> Even so, I have noticed one thing, at least, that is good. It is good for people to eat, drink, and enjoy their work under the sun during the short life God has given them, and to accept their lot in life. And it is a good thing to receive wealth from God and the good health to enjoy it. To enjoy your work and accept your lot in life—this is indeed a gift from God. God keeps such people so busy enjoying life that they take no time to brood over the past.[9]

Eat, drink, and enjoy your work. Accept your lot in life and enjoy the life you have rather than yearn for one you do not—that's the real gift of God. You don't have to attach some deeper meaning to your work. You don't need to analyze every move you make, wondering how it fits into some higher calling or greater purpose. "Enjoy what you have rather than desiring what you don't have. Just dreaming about nice things is meaningless—like chasing the wind,"[10] the writer of Ecclesiastes adds in the next chapter. In other words, it's okay to settle for what you have, no matter how ordinary it may be. Enjoy where you are and what you are doing. If it doesn't look Instagrammable to others, who cares? It's your life. Enjoy it.

The writer of Ecclesiastes sums it up like this:

> So I recommend having fun, because there is nothing better for people in this world than to eat, drink, and enjoy life. That way they will experience some happiness along with all the hard work God gives them under the sun.[11]

9. Ecclesiastes 5:18–20.
10. Ecclesiastes 6:9.
11. Ecclesiastes 8:15.

The writer isn't giving us a license to live hedonistic lives. Instead, he gives us permission to be content and enjoy, truly enjoy, the life God has given us whether we have a lot or a little, live in our dream house or have settled for a cramped old house with squirrels in the walls.[12] In a world filled with frustrated, discouraged, and angry people, this is the dream life.

### A Final Word for Those Who Feel Like They Have Let Their Parents or God or Themselves Down with Their Life Choices

If you want your life to count, keep these two commandments: Love God and love people. It's never too late to start. Your choices in the past might have wrecked your life, but God's grace is bigger than your wrecks. Wherever you are, whatever you have done in the past, start today by loving God with everything that is in you and putting that love into action by loving others in tangible ways. The Bible is filled with examples of how to do both. If you are unsure how to get started, read the short letter called 1 John.

*But I've let God down so many times,* you might say, *and my parents are really disappointed in the direction of my life, and to be honest, I'm not too thrilled with where I am either.* More people have been in your shoes than you might imagine. Where you are now is less of the issue than where you go from here. The first step I've already mentioned. Love God. Love others. If you find yourself in a dead-end job, loving God and loving the people with whom you work can make it better. The same goes with whatever situation you may be in. Then seek help with

12. The voice of experience.

the messes in which you find yourself, either from counselors or financial advisers or others who have walked your path and have come out safely on the other side. Is this overly simplistic advice? Yes. But it works. Love God. Love people. Seek help. Where you are now is not the final chapter of your life. The big question is where you go from here.

## FOUR

# Did Not Allowing My Children to Watch *The Simpsons* Make Any Difference?

In the interest of full disclosure, I must admit that the line my wife and I drew in the sand over what our children could or could not watch was not, in fact, *The Simpsons*. I used *The Simpsons* in the title only because first-run episodes have appeared continuously on Fox since 1989, which makes it relevant-ish for today's parents as well old goats like myself whose children are approaching forty. No, the actual thing that we forbade our children from watching and which also embarrassed them when they had to tell their friends during a sleepover that no, they could not watch that movie, was in fact, *The Mighty Ducks*. I'll pause while you grab a towel to wipe up coffee that you just spit all over this book while laughing.

*Why* The Mighty Ducks, you might ask. It was, after all, a Disney movie. It was so Disney that when Disney was awarded ownership of an expansion hockey team, they named it the

Mighty Ducks of Anaheim. You can't get much more Disney than that! Disney in the 1990s equaled wholesome and safe for parents. We owned VHS tapes of nearly every kids' movie released between roughly 1988 and 1999. Those we didn't own, we rented. We rented Disney's *Wild Hearts Can't Be Broken* so many times that I still see horses jumping off of diving boards in my sleep. *Horses doing what?!* you might ask, which only means a) you were not a young girl in 1992; or, b) you did not have a daughter of a certain age that same year. We had three, which meant we were Disney's target audience, a role we gladly accepted except when it came to *The Mighty Ducks*.

Again, what was the big deal with *The Mighty Ducks*? Two things: timing and attitude. When the movie hit home video and thus became a must-watch at most kids' sleepovers, our children were at the age where our focus as parents had shifted away from actions to attitudes. From all we had read and heard in conversations with other parents, we felt like the attitudes the kids in the movie displayed were not ones we wanted copied in our home. If you have children between the ages of five and twelve, you get what I am saying. Also, we read that the kids in the movie used words we did not want our kids repeating. It's not like they had never heard bad language, but it was different coming from the mouths of other children. Put it all together, and that is why when our daughters asked if they could rent *The Mighty Ducks* from our local video store or watch it at a friend's house, our answer was always no. Of course, our children smiled and said, "Okay, Dad, you know what's best. I'm thrilled with your decision." Hahahaha. Perhaps that happened in a parallel universe. In the one in which I live, my saying no was always met with eye rolls and moans and "Why? What's so bad about *The Mighty Ducks*!?"

Honestly, I think every time we said no to this movie, our girls had to wonder if their parents had any idea what they were doing. So did I.

## Too Much Credit, Too Much Blame

When I started writing long ago, I promised myself I would never write a book on parenting. I don't know how anyone writes on that topic, at least more than once. I realized I had no idea what I was doing as a parent within the first twenty-four hours of bringing our first child home from the hospital. She started crying in the middle of the night, and nothing my wife and I did could get her to stop. And we had many things to try because we'd read every book out there on child development and soothing babies and everything else. The books all felt useless in the wake of a baby who refused to stop crying at 2:00 a.m. We soon became desperate.

Before our first child was born, we made a bold pronouncement that our children would never have a pacifier. The sight of three- and four-year-olds walking around the grocery store with a binky in their mouths led to that big parenting decision. Our children would not be like that, we declared. And then came that first night alone with our child. Nearly four decades later, I can still see my wife walking to our kitchen that night with something in her hand while I frantically rocked our four-day-old daughter, singing softly or shushing or I don't know what. A few moments later, my wife placed a pacifier in our daughter's mouth. Our baby girl immediately stopped crying and was soon asleep. So much for our bold pronouncement of how we were going to be different parents, i.e., better than those who resorted to things like pacifiers to keep their children from crying.

My experience on that first night of actually caring for a child pretty much set the tone for the rest of my parenting experience. If you are a parent, you know exactly what I mean. I think life as a parent really comes down to having every "I will never . . ." or "My child will never . . ." statement we have ever made shredded before our very eyes, and us along with them. It is like trying to keep Godzilla from stomping all over Tokyo. The army may have the perfect plan, but it always falls apart before the king of the monsters is completely out of the water of Tokyo Bay. Am I saying children are as destructive as Godzilla? Of course not. He's a lightweight compared to what kids can do to a parent. Of course I'm kidding. Sort of.

This is all to say that even with five adult children, I do not claim to be an authority on parenting. I do not write this chapter to make you feel guilty over your perceived failures, nor do I write it to give you some sort of secret formula that will guarantee your kids will turn out exactly the way you pray they will. When it comes to parenting advice, this is all I really have: When children turn out well, I believe parents get too much credit. And when children do not, I believe parents get too much blame.

I came to this conclusion thanks to my late friend Don Holt. Don had one of the softest, most compassionate hearts of anyone I have ever known. Of course, I got to know him after he was released from prison. Don had only served a small portion of his four-hundred-year sentence when he was released. That's not a typo. The Oklahoma County District Attorney convinced a judge and jury to hand down a four-hundred-year sentence. It made for good headlines in the paper. This wasn't Don's first trip behind bars. Before I got to know him, he had been a career criminal who, by his own admission, deserved to be locked up and have the key thrown away. He also had a sibling who was a pastor. And another who was an engineer. All grew up in the same household with the same set of rules and the same parents. How is that possible? I'm sure his mother asked herself that question every night.

## We Need Some Sort of Advice

Although I promised myself I would never write a book on parenting, I read several during the course of my parenting career. Historically, books on parenting were a foreign concept until Dr. Benjamin Spock penned *The Common Sense Book of Baby and Child Care* in 1946. His book was a reaction to the very stern model of parenting born on the frontier, where children were expected to do chores on the farm within a few weeks of being born.[1] Instead of strict and, for the child's backside, painful discipline, Dr. Spock recommended a more gentle and nurturing model of parenting. I don't know if it was his approach that made his book popular, or just the fact that for the first time parents had an instruction manual for raising children—and someone to blame if the kids turned out bad—but the book sold like crazy. It was a cultural phenomenon. Of course, with his book coming out in 1946, Dr. Spock became *the* guide for the parents of the baby boom. If you don't like how Boomers run the world, now you know who to blame.

I never read Dr. Spock, and based on how familiar I became with my father's belt as a boy, neither did my parents. By the time I became a parent in 1985, the Christian world at least had moved on to new authorities on parenting. For a couple of young parents like my wife and me, it felt like a godsend.

1. Hyperbole alert.

We first attended video seminars featuring a man we had never heard of, a guy named Dr. James Dobson. I believe the first was called *Focus on the Family* and the second was called *Turn Your Heart Toward Home*. As best I can remember, there was nothing political about these seminars. Instead, the focus was on biblical principles for raising children who would grow into responsible, well-functioning adults. Dobson had also written a book called *The Strong-Willed Child*, and since we had a couple of those in our household, my wife and I devoured that as well. We read other authors and even attended a weeklong parenting seminar that the church for whom I was working at the time required us to attend. My wife and I sat through all the sessions, but as soon as we discovered the guy teaching never had children of his own, we pretty much stopped listening. Why? I refer you to the pacifier story above. Everyone is an expert on raising children until they actually have to raise one.

We went to these seminars and read these books for the same reason that all parents read books on parenting and watch webinars on the topic. It is the same reason we did not allow our children to watch *The Mighty Ducks* when they were little and why we bought an educational video game system rather than a Nintendo. From the moment the doctor said "It's a girl" for the first time, we felt an unbelievable pressure to get this right. No parent wants to screw up their children and thus ruin any chance they may have for a happy life. More than that, we felt, again like every parent, this tremendous responsibility to do everything within our power to set up our children for success in life. This same pressure is what makes young parents more than a little insane over trying to get their two-year-old into an elite preschool. How will little Suzy ever get into a top medical school if she attends a preschool where they don't offer Latin along with finger painting?[2]

And then there's the fear. Every parent feels it. The fear of the big bad world that's waiting out there to rob our children of their innocence and undo everything we try to do for them. The fear of the bad influences waiting on the school bus and in the classroom and on the playground. "Bad company corrupts good character" 1 Corinthians 15:33 says, and we know there's a lot of bad company out there. We've experienced it ourselves. Now all we want to do is protect our kids from it because we also fear the bad choices our children might make. Our fear is not misplaced. We know from experience the lifetime scars inflicted by every poor life choice. We want better for our kids. That is why we do what we can to protect our children's innocence and burgeoning faith. Rules are more than rules. They're guardrails for our children's own protection.

Worse than the fear is the guilt. A forty-year veteran of parenting talking here: You will experience guilt over many of your parenting decisions. That's how parenting works. The harder you try to be a good parent, the more you will feel like an absolute failure. It doesn't matter if your children are five or fifty. At some point, and usually these moments correspond to birthdays, holidays, weddings, or some other huge family event, you will do or say something that will hurt your child's feelings or upset them or set them off or whatever, and you will feel like the worst parent in the world. Often, and this is the loveliest part of parenting, just in case you failed to come to this realization on your own, your children will make sure to tell you that you are indeed the worst parent in the world. It's a special moment I think every parent experiences at least

2. More hyperbole.

once . . . a year, month, or day, depending on the ages of your children.

The deadly combination of responsibility, pressure, fear, and guilt is what drives us to make rules for our kids and attend seminars and read books on parenting, even books on parenting adult children,[3] and go to counseling and do everything else this tribe we call parents do to navigate our way through the adventures of parenting. To be clear, I am not in any way calling into question the value of these resources, except, of course, those written or conducted by people who have never had children of their own or those who wrote books or put together seminars before their children hit puberty.[4] In my own experience, many parenting resources have been very helpful.

However, I have also found that these resources can add to the fears and the guilt that we naturally carry around as moms and dads. Sometimes, trying to figure out what to do right feels like being slapped in the face with all that you have done wrong. Add in parenting complications like divorce or adoption or long-distance moves, and you have to be very careful not to allow what is supposed to help to turn into one more thing that makes you feel like a failure. For me, the best resource I've ever found is simply an honest conversation with other parents who are going through the same life stages and struggles that I face. Talking with fellow travelers lets you know that you are indeed normal. More than anything, that's often what we need

3. For you young parents, you only thought you were off the hook when your child goes off to college or gets married. Ha! The joke is on you. And yes, this also means that you are still a source of fear and guilt and anxiety for your parents, just as your children are for you. It's a vicious cycle that started with the birth of Adam and Eve's kids and will continue on as long as adults are crazy enough to continue having children.

4. You don't know what parenting means until massive amounts of hormones hit your child's bloodstream. It is not for the faint of heart.

to know. Your kids did this and you reacted this way and they did this in return? Yeah, I've been through that. My kids did the same thing. You are not a failure. You are normal.

## Not About How to Parent

It's been a very long time since I first had to wrestle with the choices I made as a dad. Now I often look back and wonder what difference they all made. By the grace of God all five of my daughters are basically fully functioning adults with jobs. Don Holt's mom would probably say my wife and I knocked it out of the park as parents because none of our children have spent time in a federal prison. Nor have I had to live through the heartache of a child battling addictions or any of the other nightmare scenarios far too many moms and dads have to experience. I have nothing but the greatest respect for all of you who have spent sleepless nights worrying as your greatest fears for your children have come true. Just having a functional child feels like a bridge too far for you. I pray that God's grace will surround you. I cannot fathom how your heart must ache.

As I said, I am fortunate because my children are by any measure good people. But for parents who are Christ followers, don't we long for more? Our greatest hope is that our children will embrace our faith. More than that, above all else we pray our children will love God with all their hearts. By that standard, I am a failure. Only two of my daughters openly identify as Christ followers. One other believes in God, but beyond that she's still trying to figure things out. One is an atheist and another once identified as an atheist, but now I'm not really sure what she believes. Does this change how I feel about my daughters? Not in the least. Why should it?

Here is the only piece of parenting advice I will make in this chapter: What our adult children do with the faith we did our best to live out in front of them has absolutely nothing to do with us. It's all on them. Love God or deny he exists, that's their choice. "But, but, but what about Proverbs 22:6," some may object. "It says to train up a child in the way they should go and when they are old they will not depart from it. They'll come back to the faith, you just watch." I'm not exactly sure what constitutes *old* in that passage, but I started feeling old in my midthirties. If that's the case, then I have an old child who did depart from the way and will in all likelihood never go back to it. Proverbs 22:6 is a classic verse quoted often by people who either do not have adult children or are lucky enough for their kids to have turned out exactly the way they planned. For those on the other side of hearing this Bible Band-Aid thrown out to somehow give us hope, we hear something less than encouraging. We hear a guilt inducer that says if we had trained our children right, they'd still be on that path. Since the Bible guarantees that a child trained right will turn out all right, the problem must be you, you lousy parent. The path your child is now on is not the child's fault but yours!

If you go by this logic, then the first entity not to raise their children exactly right was in fact God. He was Adam and Eve's parent, and look how they turned out! Might then we assume that the problem with this line of thinking is not in Proverbs 22:6 but in our interpretation of it, because the bottom line in raising children is there is no magic formula. You don't know how your kids will turn out. No one does.

So again, I go back to the title question. Did the choices my wife and I made as parents make any difference? Well, they did for us. No matter what life choices our children make, my wife and I can both look back and say we did our best to show our girls a life worth living. That's all any of us can really do, good parent or bad (and we are all a combination of the two). What our children do with our examples is up to them. What will inspire one child will be an excuse for another.

And this is the uncomfortable truth with which every parent must eventually come to grips. We have zero control over how our kids will turn out or the life-altering decisions they will make. We may have some influence, and our examples will shape how they view their choices, although we don't know if that influence and example will be taken positively or negatively. But we do have control over what *we* do and the choices *we* make. That is why my wife and I made the television/movie viewing decisions we did. We wanted to protect our daughters' innocence as long as we could. We knew the world is filled with enough bad that they couldn't dodge it their entire lives, but we chose to shield them as long as we could. Your children may appreciate the choices you make. They may resent them. That's on them. Not you.

## A Final Word for Weary Parents

Give yourself grace, Mom and Dad. Give yourself grace. Even if you were a less than ideal parent, your past example does not necessarily doom your children to repeat your mistakes. My dad was, by his own admission, a less than good father. After my parents' divorce when I was ten, my relationship with him went from bad to worse. Thankfully it improved over the years so that by the time he died forty years after the divorce, the two of us had the kind of relationship I had always hoped to have with him. However, long before the two of us were reconciled,

I faced a choice. I could either be just like my father or I could learn from his example and do better. I chose the latter. This is why I wrote in the chapter above that your example as a mom or dad will either be an inspiration or an excuse, depending on what your children choose to do with it. If you've blown it as a parent in the past, own your failures, seek forgiveness, make amends, then move forward. Do not let guilt over the past determine how you interact with your children today. This is the beauty of the grace of God. Every day is a new day with a new set of choices and possibilities laid out before us. If you failed yesterday, by the grace of God do better today. Then lean into his grace tomorrow until there are no more tomorrows.

# FIVE

## Is God Sort of Mean?

When I turned in the manuscript for one of my early books, I included a request for the title. My working title had been *The Prayer of Job*, which was a play on *The Prayer of Jabez*, a book that was all the rage back in those days. Jabez prayed for blessing. Job's words that inspired my book weren't exactly a prayer. They were more a statement to his wife when he said, "Should we accept only good things from the hand of God and never anything bad?"[1] If you haven't guessed, it was a book about suffering, not blessings. *The Prayer of Job* didn't exactly convey that idea, which is why when I finished the manuscript I had settled on a new title, *When God Isn't Good*.

My editor, who also happened to be a good friend, could not reject my idea fast enough. "You might as well call it *When God Isn't Holy* or *When God Isn't Love*," he shot back. He may have also said something about my title being borderline heresy. Maybe not even borderline. Advertising heresy is never a strong selling point when you are writing a general market Christian book.

1. Job 2:10.

I tried to argue the point. I wasn't saying God is not good. However, I wanted to give the book this title because for those who are going through suffering, there are times when you have serious doubts about the goodness of God. Of course, no one wants to admit that these thoughts run through our heads, and maybe for all the really good Christians out there they do not, but they have for me.

Pause.

Hold on a second.

Whew. No lightning crashed through my roof for writing that last sentence. Not that I expected it. C. S. Lewis didn't get struck by lightning when he wrote his short masterpiece, *A Grief Observed*, after the death of his wife. Both Lewis and his wife were believers. When she received her cancer diagnosis, they prayed for a miracle. At times, it appeared a miracle was on its way. But then, as he wrote, "Step by step we were 'led up the garden path.' Time after time, when (God) seemed most gracious He was really preparing the next torture."[2] That roller coaster of hope followed by devastation led him to wonder, "What reason have we, except our own desperate wishes, to believe that God is, by any standard we can conceive, 'good'?"[3] Lewis made this statement early in his struggle with grief, although this sentiment was not his final say on the matter. Yet, his feelings are exactly what many experience as they go through the worst that life has to throw at us.

I think if Lewis had been my editor, he would have loved my title. But he wasn't, and so my fifth book was called *Out of the Whirlwind*. I never cared for that title because it communicated absolutely nothing about what the book was actually about. A

2. C. S. Lewis, *A Grief Observed* (Harper San Francisco, 1961, 1996), 30.
3. Lewis, *A Grief Observed*, 29.

later, revised edition with another publisher came closer. They gave it a title that at least gave the reader an idea of what they were about to read: *How Can a Good God Let Bad Things Happen?* Neither edition sold particularly well, although the first incarnation was a finalist for a Christian book award. Maybe if I'd written a book called *How Can a Good God Do Anything but Shower You with Everything You Ever Wanted?* it might have become a bestseller. However, I find that title to be borderline heresy. Maybe not even borderline.

This is the tension with which many of us live. The God we want is the good God who gives us every good thing. And he does that. Jesus himself said in Matthew 7:11, "If you sinful people know how to give good gifts to your children, how much more will your heavenly Father give good gifts to those who ask him." But there are times when God seems to be, in Lewis's words, a God who sets us up for the next torture. Job's wife had had enough of that God when she told her husband to go ahead and curse God and die. Her words don't seem over the top when you consider that she too had just witnessed the deaths of all ten of her children. Lest we think that Job is some sort of outlier, we find the same anguish throughout the Bible, including from the mouth of Jesus himself when he cried out from the cross, "My God, my God. Why have you abandoned me?"[4]

So which picture of God is correct, the God who gives good gifts to his children in Matthew 7:11 or the God who forsakes his only Son in Matthew 27:46? I'm sorry, but that's not the question I plan to answer in this chapter. To be completely honest, I'm not even here to answer the title question with a simple yes or no. I'll leave it to you to wrestle with both of those questions on your own. Now who's being mean?

4. Matthew 27:46.

The genesis of this chapter began not with a deep-seated question about God's character that perhaps carried over for the past ten-plus years after watching my father die but with a far more innocuous activity. I was reading the Bible one day and I came across a passage that I had read hundreds of times before. However, on this particular day, something about the verses in front of me jumped off the page. I actually said to myself, *Whoa! Does that mean what it sounds like it means? If it does, God sounds kind of mean.*

Now, wait a minute, you're probably thinking. The Bible, when read properly, should not breed doubts about God's character. God's Word chases our doubts away. The Bible is his love letter to us, the handbook for living, the owner's manual for the human soul, the source of all our comfort. You read the Bible to feel better when you are feeling bad, not to feel worse when you are feeling good. The Bible produces faith, not questions. If reading the Bible makes someone doubt God's character, then, then, then . . . uh, there's something wrong with you, Mr. Doubting Thomas! You just have to keep digging deeper. Read those verses in their context. For that matter, read the notes at the bottom of the page of some study Bible. That should clear everything up. If you read the Bible in a way that makes God sound mean, you aren't reading it right.

Or are you?

Again, this chapter is not about God's character. This chapter is really about the mental gymnastics many of us go through to align the uncomfortable parts of the Bible with our preconceived ideas about God. I do not believe God is in any way offended with us wrestling with the questions Lewis raised in *A Grief Observed*. I recommend reading that small book in its entirety to understand how Lewis worked through his grief while holding on to his faith. I know God is not offended by such questions because he never struck anyone dead in the Bible for asking them. When Jeremiah poured out his broken heart to God and accused God of deceiving him, the Lord responded with compassion, not condemnation.[5]

However, I believe the God who created heaven and earth is deeply offended by our often sincere efforts to explain away the hard passages of the Bible and thus remake his image into something more palatable. The process reminds me of when my daughters entered their dating years. At some point they'd all bring their latest boyfriends to the house to meet my wife and me. And our dachshund, Frank. Frank hated teenage boys. Man, I miss that dog. Anyway, they'd bring a boy over to the house for dinner or just to meet us, and from time to time, the young man in question would make a less than favorable first impression not only with Frank but with my wife and me. After the kid left, our daughters always asked, "So, what did you think?" We didn't have to answer. The looks on our faces gave us away. On those occasions, our daughters inevitably said, "You don't know him like I do. He's really . . ." and she'd list off all his wonderful qualities we happened to miss.

I always found this process wildly humorous and entertaining until my wife confessed that she had to do the same thing with me. *Had* is not the right word. *Has* is closer to the truth. Apparently she still has to explain me to some of her friends because I often don't make a great first impression. Even with those I do know, I have an expiration date. I can only take so much of people until I need to be alone with a book, either writing or reading. That's probably because deep down, I'm a socially awkward introvert who can get up in front of a huge

5. Jeremiah 20.

crowd and never think twice about it, but if I have to mingle with that crowd afterward, I will be very quiet and guarded, and the look in my eyes will tell you that I cannot wait to get out of there. With people I know and love, I'm completely the opposite. Yet the first doesn't cancel out the second nor the second the first. Both are who I am. If you want to have a relationship with me, you don't get to pick and choose between the different parts of who I am. If you want me, this is what you get.

I think the last sentence is pretty much a universal sentiment. Love me for who I am, not who you want me to be, because if you choose the latter, you will always be disappointed. If this is true of human relationships, how much more so should it be for the divine? One of our taglines to explain the faith to unbelievers is that Christianity is not about religion but about a relationship. For any relationship to work, both parties have to be honest, with one another and with themselves. If not, everything will soon fall apart.

All of this brings me to the passage that started the conversation with myself that led to this chapter, John 12:37–40:

But despite all the miraculous signs that Jesus had done, most of the people still did not believe in him. This is exactly what Isaiah the prophet had predicted:

> "Lord, who has believed our message?
> To whom has the Lord revealed his powerful arm?"

But the people couldn't believe, for as Isaiah also said,

> "The Lord has blinded their eyes
> and hardened their hearts—

so that their eyes cannot see,
    and their hearts cannot understand,
  and they cannot turn to me
    and have me heal them."

Look closely at what the passage says. "They couldn't believe
. . . the Lord has blinded their eyes and hardened their hearts."
In other words, no matter how many times these people came
to see Jesus speak in person, no matter how many miracles
they saw him perform or how many parables they heard him
tell, they always walked away in the exact same spiritual condi-
tion they were in when they first arrived, because the Lord had
blinded their eyes and hardened their hearts. Now let me ask
you a very honest question, and it's just us, so it's okay: Does
this sound fair? All our lives we're told that God is love. We
hear it in church. We hear it in Christian music. We hear it in
Super Bowl commercials. Even people who have never darkened
the door of a church but who have some nominal belief in God
would most likely tell you that the God of their nominal belief
is love.

I ask you, does "The Lord has blinded their eyes and hardened their hearts" sound loving? Let's be honest and go ahead
and say what we are all thinking: NO! Love means second
chances and third chances and fourth chances and as many
chances as it takes for someone to turn it around. That's how
love looks on a human level. So if God is love, then there has
to be a very good reason why he blinded these people's eyes
and hardened their hearts.

There has to be.

The default explanation that I've heard more times than I
care to count is that God only hardened the hearts of those
whose hearts were already hard and were not going to turn

anyway. He blinded the eyes of those who, even if they could see, would never let their eyes be pried open to the truth in front of them. God in his infinite knowledge already knew how these people were going to respond to Jesus, which is why he left them the way they were. Yes, they could not turn to Jesus, but they weren't going to anyway.

Whew. Now I feel better, and God looks a lot better. He is just giving those people what they deserve (no argument on that one, which we will explore in greater detail in a moment), no more, no less.

Except . . . that's not what this passage says, either in John or in Isaiah, which John quotes. Both describe a group of people with whom God has lost all patience. There are no more second chances. For generations he offered those chances, but no more. It's judgment time. For those who witnessed Jesus's miracles and remained unmoved, what they had seen only made them that much more accountable for their actions, not less.

*But they couldn't believe,* we argue.

And the point is?

*But that's not fair, not if God is love,* we protest.

Unfortunately, God's actions are fair. They are the very definition of fair because fairness is giving people what they have coming. Aka, justice.

*But they didn't have a chance to turn their lives around,* we still say.

Again, the point is what?

*This seems so harsh.*

Don't worry. It gets worse.

One of the most troubling passages in the Bible comes immediately after one of the most encouraging. Romans 8 is often referred to as the high-water mark of the Bible. This is the chapter where we hear such promises as verse 28, which says, "And we know that God causes everything to work together for the good of those who love God and are called according to his purpose for them." The entire chapter is like a greatest hits of all the best parts of the Bible. Chapter 8 tells us that if God is for us, who can be against us, and nothing can separate us from God's love.[6] If Romans 8 were a football halftime speech, it is the kind that motivates a team to overcome a forty-two-point deficit and win the game.

And then comes chapter 9.

Romans 9 is not a downer chapter by any means. Theologically, it is every bit as rich as Romans 8. However, chapter 9 also contains a couple of sections that send us scrambling for explanations, none more so than verses 10–13:

> Not only that, but Rebekah's children were conceived at the same time by our father Isaac. Yet, before the twins were born or had done anything good or bad—in order that God's purpose in election might stand: not by works but by him who calls—she was told, "The older will serve the younger." Just as it is written: "Jacob I loved, *but Esau I hated*." (NIV, emphasis added)

Some translations like the New Living soften the blow by rendering the last verse, "I loved Jacob, but I rejected Esau." However you choose to translate the final phrase, the word used in the original language has only one primary meaning: hate, detest. So what are we to make of that!?

Paul, the writer of Romans, did not coin the phrase "Jacob I loved but Esau I hated." The Old Testament prophet Malachi did in the first chapter of the book that bears his name. These

---

6. Romans 8:31, 38–39.

aren't Malachi's words, either. The prophet speaks as a mouth-piece of God, which means these are the Lord's words. As such, these words don't just refer to Isaac and Rebekah's twin boys. They also apply to the nations that came from each of them. Jacob was the father of the nation of Israel, of whom God says through Malachi, I have always loved you. The Edomites came from Esau. God says the Edomites should be called "The People with Whom the Lord Is Forever Angry."[7] Forever. Angry. I recommend pausing and allowing those words to sink in for a moment.

Now for the question that someone very close to me asked over and over and never liked any answer I ever gave: How can God be love and still hate Esau? Romans 9 makes it very clear that this choice was made before either Jacob or Esau was even born. God's decision had absolutely nothing to do with the "works" of either one and had everything to do with God's freedom to do what he wants to do as God. In other words, as Paul puts it a little later in the chapter,[8] God is God and who are we to argue?

*I know what you're doing*, some might protest. *This is one of them there Calvinist verses my preacher warned me about.* This sort of argument is an easy out that prevents us from allowing the Bible to speak. Words like *Calvinist* or *Arminian* carry very little meaning for most people and are instead boogeymen to warn us away from hard-to-understand passages.

Leaving the boogeymen to boogey off on their own, we're still left with a very difficult passage to wrap our minds around. Like the passages from John and Isaiah, something about it strikes us as unfair. Romans 9:10–13 makes it sound

7. Malachi 1:4.
8. Romans 9:19–21.

as though God does what God wants to do, leaving us with no say in the matter. No one wants to hear that. I know I don't. I had a professor back in my Bible college days who tried to find a way around such unpleasantries. Referring to election in this passage, he said to us in a thick, Yazoo City, Mississippi, drawl, "Now this is what you have to understand about election. You see, God casts a vote for you. And the devil casts a vote against you. But you, you cast the deciding vote." Ahhh, this is a much nicer idea. It's like we get to go into that voting booth, draw the curtain closed, and make up our own mind. God hopes we will vote with him. Of course, the devil is sitting out there, counting on us to vote with him. But however we vote, we're the ones who make the decision. This is a great explanation for a difficult passage, except it has absolutely nothing to do with what Romans 9:10–13 actually says.

No matter how much I may hope that my voice will count in my eternal election, the passage doesn't tell me that I have the final say in the matter. I don't have the space nor is it my inclination to try to do a deep dive into questions about God's sovereignty and human free will, questions that have filled theology books for the past two millennia. Instead I want to ask this question, one that is really the driving force behind this chapter: If Romans 9 is true, and if this is who God is, will you still believe? If the God in the Old Testament who ordered the extermination of nations as a form of judgment after waiting hundreds of years for those nations to turn to him, if these Old Testament stories are true, will you still believe? If God loves Jacob and hates Esau, will you still believe? Or must you find a way around such unpleasantries, in effect giving God a makeover, before you will believe and trust in him?

These are in no way academic questions. They go to the very heart of what it means to be a follower of Jesus Christ. One of the first lessons taught in the first chapter of the Bible is simply this: God made us in his image. We don't get to re-make him into ours. No matter what our motivation may be, explaining away the hard passages of the Bible is another way of conforming God into the image of what we want him to be rather than loving him for who he is. We read that God is love and make up our own minds about what that is supposed to mean. We then explain away the hard verses that contradict our understanding of love rather than allowing these hard verses to inform and shape our understanding of the term.

Where then does this leave us? Wary, I hope, wary of embracing ideas about God that are not consistent with who he says he is in the Bible. In Romans 1, Paul lays out the case for how all the world needs the forgiveness and grace that can only be found in Jesus. Human beings weren't always so distant from God. But we refused to worship God as God, or even give him thanks. Instead, the human race thought up foolish ideas of what God is like.[9] We might be tempted to think that Paul was only talking about the idols that filled temples in the ancient world. *Who could be so foolish as to worship a piece of stone?* we like to say two thousand years later. Yet when we remake God into what we want him to be, are we any different? Explaining away difficult passages to make God more palatable is, in the words of Job, "defending God with lies."[10] Job also goes on to issue a warning we would be wise to heed: "What will happen when he finds out what you are doing?"[11]

9. Romans 1:21.
10. Job 13:7.
11. Job 13:9.

God doesn't need to be defended, only embraced. He is holy, not safe. His holiness elicits fear in those who are accustomed to always making excuses for bad behavior, but what else should we expect when the fear of the Lord is the beginning of wisdom? God is just, and justice always appears cruel to co-conspirators.

## A Final Word for Those Who Struggle to Reconcile the Goodness and Perceived Cruelty of God

In the final chapter of *A Grief Observed*, C. S. Lewis writes:

> My idea of God is not a divine idea. It has to be shattered from time to time. He shatters it himself. He is the great iconoclast. Could we not almost say that this shattering is one of the marks of His presence? The Incarnation is the supreme example; it leaves all the previous ideas of the Messiah in ruins. And most are "offended" by the iconoclasm; and blessed are those who are not.[12]

I cannot think of a better way of summing up what I hoped to accomplish with this chapter. Our ideas about God are not necessarily the same as God's ideas about himself. Nothing shatters the former to make way for the latter quite like an honest reading of the Bible.

Does this mean we must jettison all our ideas about the goodness and mercy of God? Of course not. Our goal should always be to allow our ideas to be shaped by the Bible rather than allowing our understanding of the Bible to be shaped by our preconceived ideas.

12. Lewis, *A Grief Observed*, 66.

This exercise moves out of the realm of the theoretical when we go through suffering. In the midst of losing a loved one or a job or a marriage, it can at times be very difficult to understand how a good God could let such a thing happen. Worse yet are those moments when someone tells us that if we just had a little more faith, our loved one would not have died or our job would still be ours or our marriage would remain strong. Job's friends told him the very same thing in their conversations that are the book of Job. I think people like this come out of the woodwork and feel obligated to inform us of our own failings because they are afraid the same fate may befall them. They have to place the blame on you because to blame God is unthinkable.

The struggle to reconcile God's goodness and all the bad that befalls us is a very old battle. I explore this struggle in depth in my book *How Can a Good God Let Bad Things Happen?* The book is out of print, but copies can still be found. I cannot summarize the book in a paragraph or two. I simply recommend that you find a copy and read it. And this is not a ploy by which I can make more money off of sales of another of my books. Authors do not make money off out-of-print books, but we do find great joy if something we wrote years ago can help someone today.

## SIX

# If I Believe God Is in Control, Why Am I So Upset About the Last Election?

The title question is one with which I have wrestled since a late night of watching election results in November 1992. It was a three-way race between the incumbent who I believed to be a genuinely good man, a small Texas oilman who had no chance of winning but that was beside the point, and the governor of a small southern state who lacked, in my humble opinion, moral fiber.[1] I sat on my sofa, my jaw hanging down, unable to force my brain to accept what my eyes saw. The guy whose campaign was such a long shot that he resorted to playing the saxophone on a late-night talk show was now the president-elect. I thought America had just made a horrible mistake. I was upset and making no secret of that fact until my wife came into the room and asked me a simple question: If you believe God is in control, why are you so upset about the election results?

1. Bonus points if you recognized this reference to the movie *O Brother, Where Art Thou?*

In the thirty-plus years since that night, I have watched many elections unfold. Some years I have heeded my wife's words. Others, well, nobody's perfect. As I sat down to write this chapter, the nation was once again on the precipice of a major election. However, by the time this book is released, that election will be over and I'm not sure how I will react to the results. That is why I have written the chapter in the form of a letter to my future self. It's okay if you read my mail. That's pretty much the idea.

Dear Future Me,

Hopefully this letter finds you happy and of sound mind. In other words, I hope you survived this latest election cycle without losing your mind since your mind is my mind and I hope for both of our sakes you kept yourself together through the insanity that is and will always be American politics. I'd start this letter the same way if we lived two hundred years ago because no matter how off the rails the last election may have been, it cannot compare to 1824, when none of the four candidates received the necessary electoral votes to declare victory. The election was tossed to the House of Representatives, who elected John Q. Adams over Andrew Jackson although Jackson won the popular vote. The decision wasn't too popular with Jackson, but I digress.

I write this letter to remind you of the promise Past Me made in 1992 to stop getting upset over election results, but we both know that Past Me made promises that Present Me and Future Me are not so sure about. Past Me really believed we'd have flying cars by now. *The Jetsons* had flying cars, and Past Me believed that was the future. But then again, Past Me was eight years old, so we can probably let that slide. But Present Me is still hopeful. I saw a news story about flying cars just yesterday. Some AI program created a video of a flying Mustang. I love Mustangs, and one that flies is even better. However, I'm guessing that in every future, I still don't have one.

Speaking of AI, has it taken over the world yet, Future Me? That's all the buzz here in the present. Everywhere you turn is another story about how AI is taking over movies and television and schools and factories and driving and everything else you can think of. Has it finished the job yet, there in the future? I know you won't read this letter until this book comes out about a year after I wrote it, Future Me, but a year is a long time when it comes to robotic algorithms with a lust for power. I have to admit that I appreciate AI's benevolent side, like when the algorithm that lives in my car automatically plots a course to the nearest Mexican restaurant whenever I leave work. Is AI still nice like this, there in the future, or has its drive for power cast aside all pretense of benevolence and enslaved the human race like in *The Matrix*? Of course, most people in *The Matrix* didn't notice or didn't care that they'd been enslaved, and I suspect that's how real people would react. As long as our robot overlords pump us full of whatever we want, even if it's just an illusion, most people are happy with that.

Which brings me back to the last election. I know Past Me promised that we were never going to yell at the television again over election results. However, we both know (and please don't tell Past Me) that we haven't been the greatest at keeping this promise to ourselves. We may not have yelled, so technically I guess we kept the promise, but all three of me, Past, Present, and Future, know that the only reason I didn't yell is because on many occasions I felt more than a little dead inside over who the American people chose to be the leader of the free world.

And that's really why anyone gets upset over election results, even down to a classroom election for hall monitor. We expect more of our fellow citizens. Back in grade school social studies, when we first learned about how our democratic republic is supposed to work, I for one came away thinking that elections were about what was best for our community and state and nation as a whole. The words of John F. Kennedy's inaugural address were still fresh back then, made even more poignant by his being taken away so early in his presidency. "Ask not what your country can do for you," he said, "ask what you can do for your country." That's the essence of democracy, we were taught back in the dark ages. All of us, every American, is in this together. We may not agree with one another on everything, but we were taught that we can agree that all of us want what is best for the country as a whole. I know, I know, Past Me was more than a little naïve, but that sense that there exists a moral ideal of what America means, an ideal that all of us are striving to achieve, still flickers down deep inside. But how many election nights have gone by where that ideal dies a little more? That's what upsets us. We get mad not only because our guy lost but also because of what our guy represented, at least in our eyes: truth, justice, and the American way!

We hate to interrupt, Present Me, but both Past and Future Me are pretty sure that's Superman's line. Last time we checked, Clark Kent isn't on the ballot.

But that doesn't mean he shouldn't be! Isn't this the ideal we deserve? Ronald Reagan in his farewell address called us a city on a hill, a light to all other nations of the possibilities freedom brings as we all work together. That's inspiring stuff, the kind that makes you want to hum "The Star-Spangled Banner" or perhaps "Kum Ba Yah."

Yet we rarely see this ideal play out in actual elections. People regularly vote more out of their own self-interest than the common good. What's best for the whole means little if that doesn't translate into a better life for me. If we're honest, that's what most people are looking for when they step into a voting booth. Elections are won or lost over the state of the economy on election day. What's in it for me overrides every other concern! Whew.

Dear Future Me, I apologize for that last rant. I stepped away from the keyboard for a few minutes to calm myself down. Do I still go on rants like this in the future? I hope not. I hope that by the time you read this, I will have the self-discipline not to let fantasies of how things ought to be hijack the reality of what actually is. Of course people vote out of their own self-interest. That's human nature. Even the most altruistic among us struggles with putting the needs of others above ourselves 100 percent of the time. The country may stretch from sea to shining sea, but it is hard to look beyond our own little corner and what's happening in it.

As a result, I, like most people, have an innate sense that what is best for me and my little world will probably be best for everyone. I know this thought is as naïve as Past Me's ideas about flying cars, but it also feels like a default setting for the human brain. As small children, we naturally assume that our lives are pretty much normal and that others' lives look a lot like our own. Maturity comes as we realize how different everyone's life experiences are, as well as their greatest needs. I cannot get upset when people vote out of their self-interest because ultimately we all do.

Why I get upset over election results is not the real question I had for you, Future Me. Perhaps I have danced around the question because I know it opens me up to a wrestling match that I suspect you will have to fight as well. The question I don't want to face is not about election results but is instead a question about faith. Do I believe God remains in control when elections don't go my way? And when I get upset over the outcome, do I believe God shares my outrage?

Now, Future Me, I don't know how you reacted to your last election. I don't even know if you voted. I have no idea who won. To be honest, writing this six months before the general election, I am so sick of this election cycle that I am ready to move out of the country until it is over. It's not just the presidential election that has worn me out. As you must remember, Future Me, although I am doing my best to shove these memories out of my head so that you don't have them in yours, the commercials for our state and local elections started running before the previous Christmas. Our primary was in May. I could not keep track of all those who threw their hats in the ring to become our next governor. They all looked and sounded the same. One guy led off every commercial by telling us that his grandpappy was a preacher, as if that means anything at all about anyone other than his dear old grandpa. Another candidate (or maybe it's the same one?) promised to stop China from brainwashing our children with TikTok. That had to be the most pressing issue here in the Hoosier state. And every candidate's commercial sounded as though the US is going to hell in a handbasket, whatever that means. Kigali sounds better every day.

I wonder if God grows weary of all this election noise. I've only been on this earth for fifteen presidential cycles, and for me, every campaign sounds like a variation of all the ones before. *I'm going to get tough on crime. I'm going to solve immigration. I'm going to fix our schools. I'm going to create jobs. I'm going to sweep out corruption. And my opponent is a horrible individual, a pro-crime, anti-American subhuman career politician who never helps old ladies across the street and possibly ate a dog.*[2] If I hear one more commercial, my head might explode! I can only imagine how God must feel, having sat through the human race's attempts to find a way to govern itself since time began.

Lots of candidates invoke God's name. Those on both sides of the political aisle often claim to be people of faith. Does God love these candidates more? If the dear old grandpappy of the candidate who ran for governor here in my home state has already passed on, I wonder if Grandpa regularly lobbied the Almighty to bless his beloved grandson's campaign. Since the guy lost, I guess dear old grandpappy was too busy rollerblading on streets of gold and forgot all about his grandson's election—or God did a hard pass on the blessing request.

And the world is large. Last time I checked, there are approximately 176 nations on earth, with roughly half having some sort of democratic system of government. With 7 billion people on the planet, that's a lot of elections for God to wring his hands over. I wonder how much sleep God loses over all these election cycles, from candidate debates to primary elections up to the general election. Throw into the mix the endless back and forth about politics and candidates and issues on media platforms, most thrown into stark terms of good versus evil, truth versus lies, in countries all over the world, and God certainly has his hands full!

2. An issue that a candidate in 2024 actually had to address. Seriously. Andrew Jackson accused John Q. Adams of playing the role of a pimp for the Russian ambassador during their 1828 rematch, so I guess dog-eating allegations aren't that far-fetched.

Of course, I am above the fray. Well, hopefully I will be when Present Me catches up to the Future Me who will read this letter someday. By then I hope to be the me who never pauses on social media posts blasting one side or the other. It's hard not to get caught up in it all in a time where anger is peddled as action steps that must be taken. After all, Jesus got mad about evil. He turned the tables over in the Temple. I'm not sure if that's the same thing as fostering permanent anger toward one political party or another, since the thing that made Jesus angry was people who had turned the worship of his Father into a way to make money. Do all the communists and socialists and Marxists and all the other evil-ists trying to take over our country make God just as mad? When we elect the "wrong" people, does God turn over some tables in heaven and wonder how his people could have gone so far astray?

Thankfully, we don't have to guess how God feels about all the machinations of human government. When God created the heavens and the earth, he didn't merely put everything in motion then step back to see how things might work out as the Deists of the eighteenth century presumed. (Many of the founding fathers of the United States were in fact Deists.) Throughout the Bible, we find God is actively involved in what takes place here on earth. Isaiah 37, the story of Assyria's invasion of Jerusalem being thwarted by God himself without a human army, makes it clear that God raises up rulers and nations for his purposes, just as surely as he causes them to fall. The flow of history does not take God by surprise. Instead, he moves it to accomplish his plans, as is shown in his words through Daniel chronicling the empires he will bring about over hundreds of years. Jesus himself, when questioned while on trial for his life, told Pilate, who claimed to hold Jesus's life in his hands, "You would have no power over me at all unless it were given to you from above."[3]

Perhaps no passage better illustrates God's sovereignty over all nations of the world than Psalm 2:1–6:

> Why are the nations so angry?
>> Why do they waste their time with futile plans?
> The kings of the earth prepare for battle;
>> the rulers plot together
> against the Lord
>> and against his anointed one.
> "Let us break their chains," they cry,
>> "and free ourselves from slavery to God."
> But the one who rules in heaven laughs.
>> The Lord scoffs at them.
> Then in anger he rebukes them,
>> terrifying them with his fierce fury.
> For the Lord declares, "I have placed my chosen king
>> on the throne
>> in Jerusalem, on my holy mountain."

I love the line, "But the one who rules in heaven laughs. The Lord scoffs at them." God doesn't fret over something as trivial as an election. He rules in heaven. He holds history in his hands. Even with all the evil that lurks deep inside every human heart, God can and will accomplish his purposes.

That is why I feel compelled to ask, If God is in control, why do we get upset when elections don't go our way?

*But it is our job to elect the best leaders we possibly can who will help advance God's causes*, one might protest.

Is it?

3. John 19:11.

When ancient Israel first asked for a king, God gave them exactly what they asked for. He had the prophet Samuel anoint a man named Saul who looked like a king and who was built like a king and who carried himself like a king. In the end, Saul turned out to be a disaster. What the people wanted and what they needed were not at all the same. As the old saying goes, be careful what you wish for, especially when it comes to those entrusted with leading a nation.

*But that's why we have to choose godly leaders, especially as Christ followers in a democracy,* some might say. Unfortunately, godliness is apparently in the eye of the beholder. In the final election before I was old enough to vote, one of the leading candidates did a long interview with, of all publications, *Playboy* magazine. The interview must have been a first for *Playboy* because that candidate talked primarily about his personal relationship with Jesus Christ and being a born-again believer. That phrase had become a bit of a buzzword thanks to Richard Nixon's former hatchet man, Charles Colson, publishing his testimony in a book called *Born Again.* Not only did this candidate talk openly about his faith, he also talked about his struggles. He confessed his problems with lust and his battles with his flesh. On top of everything else, he not only attended church on a regular basis but taught a Sunday school class and had for years.

The candidate is, of course, Jimmy Carter. His image as a churchgoing, God-fearing, Southern Baptist Sunday school teacher stood in sharp contrast to the corruption and scandal of the Nixon Watergate years. And Carter won the election. People were ready for more integrity and less drama in the White House. During Carter's four years in office and throughout the decades since, he demonstrated time and again that his image was reality. The man was who he said he was, and he backed it up in the way he lived.

However, after his first term, America voted Carter out in a landslide. I have to confess, I didn't vote for him. I was young and dumb in the 1980 election, so I voted for a third-party candidate. Sticking it to the man, I think is how I put it. Since Carter lost the election, obviously many people did not vote for him. One group that not only voted for Carter's opponent, Ronald Reagan, but actively campaigned for the Republican was a large group of pastors and church members loosely organized under the banner of the Moral Majority. More than four decades later I still find myself scratching my head over this one. Carter displayed by every measure the very character these same leaders said was most important in a president, and yet they supported a man who scheduled his inauguration as governor of California in January 1967 to take place at 12:10 a.m. to take advantage of favorable astrological portents.[4] I didn't get it as an eighteen-year-old, and I don't really understand it now, not if character counts above all.

The religious right, which is more influential in politics today than ever, is far from the first group of Christians in America to band together to try to bring their influence on American life. In the late nineteenth and early twentieth centuries, the temperance movement, which was rooted in Protestant churches and led by groups like the Women's Christian Temperance Union, set out to rid America of its great evil: alcohol. Demon rum was destroying families, fueling lawlessness, and leading the country into a moral decline from which it might never recover. Their efforts ultimately led to the passage of the eighteenth

4. Steven B. Roberts, "White House Confirms Reagans Follow Astrology, Up to a Point," *New York Times*, May 4, 1988, section A, p. 1.

amendment in 1917, which was ratified in 1919. With that, Prohibition began. Booze was against the law. A new day had dawned in the nation.

Like Saul's reign over ancient Israel, outlawing alcoholic beverages was a disaster. Changing the law did not quench people's thirst. To paraphrase Romans 7, it was like Americans did not know how much they wanted a stiff drink or a cold beer until the law told them they could not have one. That's the problem with trying to usher in morality by outlawing certain behaviors. As Paul said, the law only shows us how sinful we really are. In other words, you cannot legislate morality, not that it stops anyone from trying.

Our understanding of basic human nature and the inherent sinfulness of the human race should give Christ followers a unique perspective on the political process. We know that God is on his throne. As followers of Jesus Christ, we belong to a kingdom that transcends this world. Philippians 3:20 tells us that we are citizens of heaven, while 1 Peter 2:11 reminds us that we are temporary residents and foreigners in this world, which includes whatever nation in which we happen to live. We also understand that God's grace alone, not passing new laws, can change human hearts. However, over the past four decades it seems that more and more of those who confess to believe in God's sovereignty have decided that the Almighty needs our assistance. As a result, citizens of heaven have placed their hope in the political process to bring about societal change. When that change does not come, we demonize those on the other side who are out to thwart our efforts. That's what upsets me now in the present just as it has in the past, and I know it will in the future. God is on his throne. Why do we act like he needs our help to do his job?

Does this mean we should adopt the attitude that we are just passing through this life and wash our hands of the problems of this world? Of course not! Jesus himself said his followers would feed the hungry, give water to the thirsty, invite in strangers, clothe the poor, care for the sick, and visit those in prison.[5] Whether or not we vote matters far less than living out Jesus's example.

*Surely, though, there must be something bigger we can do to impact our culture,* we might say. There is. In Romans 12:9–21, the apostle Paul lays out a game plan for how citizens of the kingdom of God can wield influence and power even within the most oppressive political systems devised by man. We know this is true because a corrupt, self-absorbed, horrible little man named Nero was ruler of the Roman Empire when Paul wrote these words. Paul never called for political action against the Romans. Instead, he called us to do something far more subversive:

> Don't just pretend to love others. Really love them. Hate what is wrong. Hold tightly to what is good. Love each other with genuine affection, and take delight in honoring each other. Never be lazy, but work hard and serve the Lord enthusiastically. Rejoice in our confident hope. Be patient in trouble, and keep on praying. When God's people are in need, be ready to help them. Always be eager to practice hospitality.
>
> Bless those who persecute you. Don't curse them; pray that God will bless them. Be happy with those who are happy, and weep with those who weep. Live in harmony with each other. Don't be too proud to enjoy the company of ordinary people. And don't think you know it all!
>
> Never pay back evil with more evil. Do things in such a way that everyone can see you are honorable. Do all that you can to live in peace with everyone.

5. Matthew 25:37–40.

Dear friends, never take revenge. Leave that to the righteous anger of God. For the Scriptures say,

> "I will take revenge;
>    I will pay them back,"
> says the Lord.

Instead,

> "If your enemies are hungry, feed them.
>    If they are thirsty, give them something to drink.
> In doing this, you will heap
>    burning coals of shame on their heads."

Don't let evil conquer you, but conquer evil by doing good.

So, Future Me, never forget that God is in control. Living out these verses is the best way to show it, no matter who won the last election.

## A Final Word for Recovering Politics Junkies

My first brush with the political process came in 1968 when my father took me to see Richard Nixon at a rally at the Oklahoma City airport. I can still remember sitting on my father's shoulders, listening to Nixon speak. When I got home, I did my first campaigning by trying to convince our next-door neighbor to vote for him. She went outside and painted the letters N-I-X-O-N on the curb and gutter in front of her house. At the time I thought I'd won my first convert to the cause. Looking back, I wonder if she was expressing a completely different opinion. I didn't consider that possibility then since I was all of six years old. Four years later my parents had split up, and my mom got remarried six weeks before the 1972 general election. I wore a "Nixon's The One" button to her wedding. Several months later I bought a Nixon wristwatch, which I still own to this day. It never kept good time. Maybe the watch was trying to tell me something.

Watergate did not destroy my love of politics. During my freshman year of college, I tried to volunteer for one of the many Republicans hoping to win the nomination to face off against Jimmy Carter. I say tried because the candidate dropped out before the Oklahoma primary election. However, with time my political zeal lessened. Once I got married and changed careers then started having children, I didn't have the time or bandwidth to worry about it as I did before. Then came that November night in 1992. That was the first time I seriously contemplated the chapter's title question, with my wife's urging. It was a moment of genuine change and freedom.

Many Christ followers feel as though we have a divine responsibility to be deeply involved in the political process. After all, as we all have heard innumerable times, America was founded as a Christian nation and we have a moral obligation to stay true to that path. Even if this concept were true, and the fact that most of the founders were Deists, not what one might consider evangelical Christians, calls this idea into question, biblically speaking we are still not called to nation building. Philippians 3:20 tells us that we are citizens of heaven, where Jesus Christ resides, not this earth. First Peter 1:1 goes on to tell us that we are strangers and aliens in this physical world. Our obligation is not to the kingdoms of this earth but to the kingdom of God.

Does this mean Christians should not vote or be involved in politics in any way? That's a question best answered by your own conscience. However, I can testify that trusting in God's sovereignty brings much greater peace than placing one's hope in an electorate made up of fallen human beings. This does not mean that the best person will always win the election, nor does it mean that a horrible person ascending to the nation's highest office has somehow thwarted God's plan. Remember, often God's most effective acts of judgment come through giving people exactly what they want and deserve. I find this truth to be chilling.

# SEVEN

# Why Don't I Feel It?

"Did you hear about what's happening down in Kentucky?" my wife asked me one evening during a commercial break from *Wheel of Fortune*. We live incredibly exciting lives.

"No. What's going on?" I asked while also wondering if I should talk to my doctor about Jardiance. I don't know what it does or what symptoms it treats, but the people singing and dancing in the commercial sure seem to enjoy it.

"Apparently a revival broke out on a Christian college campus. It started during a chapel service, and no one wanted to leave. It's been going on for a few days now," she said.

"Where did you hear this?" I asked.

"It's all over Facebook," my wife replied. By this she meant her Facebook, not mine. My social media consumption consists primarily of dachshund videos, kayaking groups, kayak trailer building groups, a couple of comedians, and my favorite baseball team. None of them had yet been impacted by a revival, although one of my kayak groups surely would have noticed if people were getting baptized in the local rivers.

"So do you think it's real or one of those Facebook things?" I asked.

My wife sort of shrugged and said something like, who knows? I nodded and went back to watching *Wheel*. It is, after all, America's game.

The following Sunday, the Kentucky awakening was all the talk at church. A handful of people had already made the three-hour drive to check it out. Others told me they planned to go in the next day or two. Me, the happenings in Kentucky slipped my mind within a few minutes of my conversation with my wife. The excitement generated by *Wheel of Fortune* does that to people.

My nonchalant approach to the awakening put me in the distinct minority among Christ followers. If the reports I heard at church were true, people were flocking to the small college in Kentucky from all over the world, all hoping to catch a little fresh fire from God. So many people made the pilgrimage that the local fire marshal nearly shut the services down because of overcrowding. I heard that the college then reserved the chapel for students only. Everyone else had to watch on video screens in other locations across campus.

The administration at the revival college eventually ended the continuous services. Finals were approaching, and life on campus had to get back to something approaching normal. I don't know what the lasting effects of the spontaneous revival may be. Again, none of the dachshund video groups I follow mentioned it on my social media feeds. The awakening also faded from my wife's Facebook rather quickly. Facebook attention spans are notoriously short.

### I Have the T-shirt

A year or so has passed since I first heard about the Kentucky awakening. I find I now watch far less *Wheel of Fortune*, but that has more to do with streaming literally anything else than it does any aftereffects of the revival. I grew bored with *Wheel* years ago, but I still watch more out of habit than anything else. I guess I'm waiting for another outrageous moment like the one back in '83 when a contestant tried solving a puzzle but failed when she said "*E.T.*" instead of "*It.*" The movie *E.T.* was all the rage back then. We howled with laughter when the big *Wheel* failure happened and keep hoping something like it will happen again.

Sometimes I wonder if attending church these days is just another habit like watching *Wheel of Fortune*. I know, I know, that's a terrible thing to say, but I don't know how else to express the feelings with which I wrestle. Spiritually, I sort of feel like I've hit a place in my Christian walk where it feels more like a treadmill than a journey. I've seen it all and I've done it all, which is why when I heard about a purported revival breaking out a mere three hours from my house, I didn't immediately jump in my car and drive down to check it out. There was a time in my life when I would have done exactly that. I don't know how or when that time passed. It's like, I don't know how to put it except to say I'm not feeling it these days. The divine spark, the spiritual tingle, the Holy Ghost giddy doesn't come over me like it once did.

Maybe I'm the odd one here. Maybe I'm the only one who is a little jaded and, dare I say it, bored in their spiritual pilgrimage, but I suspect I am not. I don't want to be jaded, and I keep trying to find a way out of the boredom, but I'm not sure what to try next. I've read all the must-read books and attended either live or on some sort of screen all the must-attend events. I prayed with Jabez back when everyone was praying with Jabez[1] and have purpose driven my life around the block a

1. *Who?* everyone under fifty asks.

time or two. I heard all about how to live my best life now, and I've loved with all five languages. I survived blood moons and the fear of being left behind. My generation got an early start on that when Hal Lindsey told us how planet earth was late and great back in the seventies and then how the eighties were the countdown to Armageddon. Spoiler alert: They weren't. I rocked with Christian rock when that was a thing and kept on rocking even when it faded into the background of the Christian subculture. I've heard more sermons than I can count on grace and faith and family and hope and relationships and discipleship and lordship and membership and every other Christian ship in the fleet and preached enough of the same myself that I pretty much know what is going to be said before the words come out of the preacher's mouth. Ecclesiastes 1:9 says there is nothing new under the sun, and the longer I walk on this Christian treadmill, the more convinced I am that Solomon must live around here somewhere.

Again, maybe it's just me who feels like this, but it's hard to know because this isn't exactly something most of us dare talk about with others. Instead, I suspect most of us who feel this way simply choose to fade away from church and other God-based activities rather than quench the excitement of all those who are feeling it. Going to church out of habit eventually loses its grip, and many formerly very committed believers end up slipping out the door and not coming back. COVID gave those feeling this way an out. Sheltering in place broke the habit, and they haven't been able to muster up the energy to reengage.

I don't want to end up like that. I don't think anyone who shares this struggle does, but there aren't a lot of attractive options. Even to admit we're wrestling with such feelings is inevitably followed by the question *What is wrong with me?*

A million years ago, my sister had a shirt that said "If God seems far away, guess who moved?" Hint: It isn't God. So if he seems far away, I am the one who has moved. In the Christian subculture we call this backsliding. That has to be the problem. If I'm not feeling it, then I must be sliding right back into the cesspool of the world. I should have gone to that revival, because that's what I need. A revival. An awakening. A jump start of Holy Spirit power to get the juices of excitement flowing back through my veins.

At least that's the prescription we assume we need. It's the prescription we hear at church. After all, I grew up singing "I've got the joy, joy, joy, joy down in my heart, down in my heart to stay." If the joy, joy, joy, joy is missing, I better find it before the devil jumps off the tack I told him to go sit on and drags me deeper down this hole. So I go back on the treadmill and crank it up to a higher setting. I read the latest must-read book and sign up for the latest must-attend event. I reset my Spotify playlist to all the latest, greatest worship songs and try to immerse myself in everything God related. I double down on the Bible reading and take extra notes during the latest week's church sermon.

And at the end of the day I . . . I . . . I can't lie. I'm still not feeling it. What's the problem?

Again, I assume the problem has to be me, so I kick in even greater effort to recreate the buzz I used to feel. Growing up I felt it a lot, especially during the week of church camp each summer. This church camp was huge. Thousands of teenagers flocked there from all over the state. And we felt it. Boy did we ever feel it. If we didn't feel it on Monday or Tuesday or Wednesday, we definitely did on Thursday. Everyone got right with God on Thursday night of church camp. Sinners got saved, and whoever was already saved made a bold declaration of rededicating their lives to Christ, almost like an annual marriage vow renewal ceremony. Everyone was crying. Everyone was singing. Everyone was different. It was great. It was the very definition of revival.

But it never lasted. Saturday morning of church camp always rolled around and everyone loaded up the church buses and went back home. A few weeks later, school started and life pretty much returned to normal. Some years we came back from camp genuinely changed. But the zip. The zing. The head over heels in love with Jesus feeling we all craved eventually faded away. By the time the next August rolled around, we were ready to get it back again. Or at least we were by Thursday night. Everyone felt it on Thursday night at church camp.

Maybe that's the problem. Maybe I need a new church camp experience.

Or do I?

### Never Meant to Last

Biblically speaking, the Thursday night at church camp feelings never last. In Exodus 14, after the Israelites crossed through the Red Sea, they stood on the shore and watched the parted waters through which they had just marched come crashing down on Pharoah and his army. Exodus 14:31 says that "When the people of Israel saw the mighty power that the Lord had unleashed against the Egyptians, they were filled with awe before him. They put their faith in the Lord and in his servant Moses." Who could ever get over experiencing something like that? You think you're about to get slaughtered by an army, then the sea opens up and the water stands on end, creating a highway for you to use to escape. Then, when the king who has enslaved your people for four hundred years tries to follow you through the water, he and his entire army are destroyed, never to be a threat to you again. To say the least, the ancient Israelites were filled with awe. They should have had enough awe to last generations, not just a lifetime.

Unfortunately, their awe had a shelf life of less than two months. It lasted exactly as long as their food supply. Once their bellies started growling, so did they. "'If only the Lord had killed us back in Egypt,' they moaned. 'There we sat around pots filled with meat and ate all the bread we wanted. But now you have brought us into this wilderness to starve us all to death.'"[2] *But that's because they didn't get it. They never got it. They only wanted the miracles. They never really believed in the One who parted the sea*, some may say. I have trouble lobbing that kind of criticism at an ancient group of people when I find myself complaining to God when a fresh crisis hits a few months after God solved the last crisis. People are people, no matter when or where they live.

We see the same thing in the New Testament. The awe everyone felt after Jesus fed five thousand lasted less than twenty-four hours. The day after the miracle, Jesus's teaching got hard. As a result, many of his disciples deserted him.[3] Sitting on the banks of the Sea of Galilee, listening to Jesus talk, literally eating a miracle, that had to feel great. But the feelings didn't last. They never do.

*But these weren't true believers*, some might say. For true believers, the feelings last forever. At least, that's what we hope. We want to feel and experience what the early church in the book of Acts felt and experienced. They saw miracles and signs

2. Exodus 16:3.
3. John 6:66.

and wonders. They felt the ground shake when they prayed. Thousands of people signed up to be a part of the Jesus movement. Everyone felt a sense of awe.[4] That's what we want to experience. That's the *it* we want to feel—more than that, the *it* we need to feel. But even in the book of Acts and even for the true believers, the feelings don't last. By Acts 7 persecution broke out against the Jesus people, and everyone had to scatter. Words like *awe* and *wonder* weren't used again to describe what Jesus's followers felt.

*Ahhh, you're making too much out of this*, some will say. Just because the word *awe* isn't used in the rest of Acts doesn't mean it was missing. Signs and wonders and miracles kept happening. At least for a while. That's what we want to experience.

Okay. I'll give you that. We all want to experience signs and wonders and miracles, unexplained phenomena that can only be described as a movement of God. And I've done that. I've seen miracles firsthand, and I'm here to tell you, the feelings don't last. The feelings sometimes don't even last through the miracles. And that's a good thing.

## A Brief Story of My Own Miracle

My wife and I had never even thought about adoption. We had three daughters already, and our youngest had just moved away to college, which meant we were by ourselves. Finally. The two of us had always been the young parents at every event. We got married when my wife was all of eighteen years old and I was the ripe old age of twenty. Three years later our first daughter was born, with another coming along two years after that and the last one two years after that. All of that means we were

4. Acts 2:43.

quite young to have an empty nest, and that was more than all right with us.

But then daughter number two spent a month in Ethiopia working in hospitals between her first and second years of medical school. On her first night in the country, she met two girls ages eleven and thirteen. Their mother had passed away about a month before, and their father had been gone for more than a decade. Long story short, my daughter actually met who would become her two youngest sisters, although it would take us nearly two years to make that happen. "Make that happen" is the wrong phrase to use, because we couldn't make anything happen. Although technically orphans, a word my daughters never used to describe themselves, my two future youngest daughters were not in an orphanage. They lived on their own in a city of over three million. I foolishly thought all I needed to do to start the adoption process was contact an adoption agency in the United States. The first call told me how wrong I was. Every agency my wife and I contacted told us the same thing: what we wanted to do was impossible. "Stop trying now before you get too deep into this," we were told, "because you are just going to end up heartbroken." It took five months and hiring a really good attorney to even come up with a list of five agencies who could possibly help us. The list was whittled down to three before we made the first call and finally down to two. The first agency explained that what we were attempting was referred to as an identified adoption, and though extremely difficult, it could be done. I thought we'd found a ray of hope until the same person informed me that they did not work with teenagers. Now down to our last hope, I called an agency in Port Angeles, Washington. "It's not impossible," the director said, "I've done it." Coincidence or miracle? You decide. All I know is our last option was our only option. Today, this agency no longer exists.

Our next coincidence or miracle came when we started filling out the first few forms of a mountain of paperwork. The form also required us to pay a $300 filing fee, the first of many fees we had to pay. About the time we filled in the last line of the first of many forms, a friend dropped by. She told us that she'd told her brother about what we were trying to do, and he wanted to help. Our friend then handed my wife three one-hundred-dollar bills.

A few weeks later we had to send in the second set of forms along with a check for $550. The day before I planned to mail it, two checks arrived from people like our friend's brother who had heard about what we were doing and wanted to help. For what it's worth, lots and lots of people knew about what we were doing because from the moment we first heard that what we were trying to do was impossible, we asked as many people as we could to pray for us. Two of those praying people sent us checks, one for $50 and one for $500. In other words, exactly what we needed.

Mystery checks kept on showing up right when we needed them throughout the adoption process. At one particular point we definitely felt the weight of "what you are trying to do is impossible." International adoption laws and rules and technicalities were in constant flux, both in the US and in Ethiopia. We reached a point in the summer of 2011 where it looked like this process was dead in the water. At the time, we were a part of an online support group of Americans trying to adopt abroad. Someone posted an update about finally being able to bring home their child from Ethiopia. I felt more than a little envious. Okay, I'll be honest. I sort of hated these people for a moment because their case was working out and ours was not. The person posting also included one little detail: the price of a one-way flight from Addis Ababa to the United States, $1,250. I'll never forget that amount. *Why?* you ask. Because the next day a letter came in the mail with no return address and no letter inside. Instead the envelope held $1,250 in cash. I knew I needed to buy two tickets, but having the exact amount for one was all the confirmation I needed not to give up.

Unfortunately, more rules changed and more requirements were added. At one point our paperwork in Ethiopia landed on the desk of a judge who glanced over it, then declared that our girls were old enough to survive on their own. Again, they were eleven and thirteen, living on their own in a city of over three million people. Our girls have an older half brother who lived with his father and stepmother. He was the one in charge of taking the paperwork to the judge. After the judge refused to sign, the brother took the paperwork back a second time and asked for a signature while a large group of people in the United States prayed fervently. The judge still said no. The brother went back again and again and again and again. The judge said no again and again and again until the brother went so many times that the judge knew there was only one way to get rid of him. She scribbled her signature across the bottom of the form and told him she never wanted to see him again. You can call that a coincidence, but this particular episode felt like we were living the story Jesus told of the unrighteous judge who finally gave in to a persistent widow. We didn't have a widow, only a persistent brother who refused to take no for an answer.

Finally, and there is much more to this story that I can bore you with if we ever meet face-to-face, we reached another impasse in the process. I don't remember exactly what ridiculous hoop was added to the adoption requirements, but this one felt fatal. Maybe it only felt like that because my father had recently passed. Before he died, he told me not to give up, that the adoption was going to happen. I wasn't so sure, and we reached a point where I pretty much knew it was not. And then I had a dream. Keep in mind that I have never been one to buy into the whole dreams and visions mumbo jumbo some groups put so much credence in. That is, until it happened to me. In my dream I was sitting on our back deck with my youngest not-yet daughter. She was asking how everything could be so green. I remember the conversation. I also remember the shirt she was wearing. It was bright yellow with short sleeves.

When I awoke it was like she was downstairs waiting for me, that's how vivid the dream was. I chalked it up to my heart making wishes until the mail came the next day with a large envelope sent all the way from Ethiopia. A missionary who kept an eye on our girls and who also managed the money we sent for food and rent and their essentials had taken our future daughters to a studio to have their portraits taken for us. When I pulled the photo out of the envelope, I nearly fell over. My soon-to-be daughter, the one with whom I had the conversation in my dream, was wearing the shirt I saw in the dream. Right then I knew I didn't need to worry. God was making the impossible happen. On the day the Super Bowl was played in Indianapolis, we brought our daughters home for the first time. When it was all over, when we were finally sitting in our living room, I felt as though I had just lived through a story in the Bible. Reading my description of the events probably won't feel that dramatic to you, and I get it. Words cannot convey the impact you experience when you live through events that feel very much like an act of God.

## The Real Question We Need to Ask Ourselves

After experiencing something so dramatic, so amazing, how am I not feeling it today? That's a great question. The hardest part of not feeling it is thinking back on how God worked through our adoption miracle, and back on all the other amazing things he has done in my life before and since, and trying to figure out why the zip and zing aren't here anymore. How can I feel bored after living through so much? How can I possibly doubt God?

The answer to the last question is easy: I don't. I don't doubt God. I don't question his power or his goodness or his grace.

You see, I now realize that the real question I face is not why am I not feeling it. The real question is why I ever thought I needed to feel it for my faith to be real! I've experienced a lot of moments where I felt like the barrier between heaven and earth had nearly ceased to exist. Those moments were great. But faith isn't about believing hard enough to feel some sort of extra spiritual zinger. Second Corinthians 5:7 says that we live by believing, not by seeing. Seeing includes feeling. When people clamored for some sign from Jesus, he told the crowds that the only sign he would give was the sign of Jonah, by which he meant that just as Jonah was in the belly of the whale for three days, Jesus was going to die, spend three days in the grave, then rise from the dead. He made good on that sign a short time later. It's a pretty good sign. Why do we think we need anything more?

Yes, there are times when my spiritual journey feels like endless treadmills of been there and done that. Isn't that about 90 percent of life anyways? Experiencing an emotional move of God is not the ultimate goal of the Christian life. Walking by faith is. When we stop feeling it, only then are we ready to truly experience the life of faith. Faith does not mean believing God for big and impossible things but simply trusting him in the mundane ordinariness of day-to-day life. You may get to experience God making the impossible come true, but be warned, you will definitely not then land in a "happily ever after" scenario. Often, the miracles we experience are there only to give us the perseverance we need to make it through the ordinary or worse that follows.

So yes, I am not feeling it. Do I have to? The biggest step of faith is trusting God completely as life plods along in the ordinary. No fireworks. No miracles. No big movement that one can point at and say, *God is moving!* Just life in all its boring ordinary-ness. Are you still in?

## A Final Word

There is no final word except to say the final paragraph is a question upon which I meditate often. Why do I follow Jesus? Is it for the giddies, the joy, the happy tingles, or is it because he is the way, the truth, and the life? If I feel nothing, if I never experience any tangible benefits from following Jesus, will I still follow? That's the question Satan posed to God about Job. It applies to all of us. Do we believe because of the benefits God gives us or do we believe because God is God? This is the million-dollar question we all must face.

## EIGHT

# Did the Church in Ancient Ephesus Have a Creative Arts Director?

It's easy to lose sight of what the church actually is in light of all the activity we usually associate with what churches do. Churches today have a lot of activities. I wonder if they did in the ancient world? I assume ancient churches had Sunday services, but I wonder if they had Sunday night services or Wednesday night prayer meetings. Did the church in ancient Ephesus have a first-century equivalent of Sunday school or children's church or middle school group meetings or high school group meetings, or did they throw all teenagers into one and call it youth group? I went to youth group long enough ago that it feels like the ancient world, since no one has called youth group youth group in about a hundred years, and instead they use names that sound cool to someone who hasn't been young enough for youth group since the Clinton administration.

I doubt if any of the ancient churches Paul helped start had bingo nights, although the book of Acts says they shared meals together, which sounds a lot like the ever-popular church pot-luck dinner, or as we call them in Indiana, pitch-ins. I wonder if pizza had been invented in time for the church in ancient Rome to have youth pizza party nights, and did any ancient churches have parents' night out or moms' night out or men's night in?

Most marriage books and seminars today quote Ephesians 5:21–33. Does that mean the ancient church in Ephesus had marriage seminars or parenting seminars? Did they conduct financial-planning seminars or seminars on how biblical creation accounts stand up to science or seminars on the end of the world? Maybe they were too far from the end of the world to worry about end-times conferences, although the church in the first century had just as much reason to assume the end was nigh as the church in the twenty-first.

Today most churches have special groups for young parents and old parents and adoptive parents and foster parents and parents without partners and partners without parents. Oh wait, that was *Sleepless in Seattle*, but it sure sounds like something a church somewhere today might offer. Did the ancient world have any sort of equivalent of men's ministries or women's ministries or children's ministries or ministries for shut-ins or shut-outs or the homeless or jobless or careless?

I doubt if first-century churches needed weight-loss groups, since most people did some sort of hard manual labor. But you can find them in churches today along with step aerobics groups and pickleball groups and bike-riding-enthusiast groups and Thursday night basketball groups and any other group you can imagine at some church somewhere.

Since electricity was still nearly two millennia away, none of the ancient churches needed a tech team or a sound team or a light team, but did they have greeter teams or chariot parking-lot teams or security teams or information teams or teams of people who wander around the foyer "looking for the bathroom" when really they were too antsy to sit through the sermon?

I guess what I'm really asking is did the church in ancient Ephesus or Corinth or Jerusalem pack their schedules with the same beehive level of activities most of us associate with churches today? If so, although I somehow doubt they did, did they find it as easy to lose sight of what the church actually is in the midst of all churches do?

I know two thousand years have passed between the first century and our own, but the essence of what the church is has not changed. Multitudes of books have been written between then and now on the role of the church and the purpose of the church and the offices of the church and the theology of the church and the ordinances of the church, which some churches prefer to refer to as sacraments, yet at its most basic level, a church is now and has always been just a group of people doing their best to love God and live like Jesus together. May be a big group. May be small. Might have a building. Might meet under a tree. Might be highly organized (or as organized as a church can be) or might be pretty loose. Doesn't matter. The one thing that ties all churches together across time and space is the understanding that a church is relational. Relational with God. Relational with those who share a passion for Jesus. The relationships tell us we aren't the only ones out there who want to know God more and that we aren't the only ones struggling with whatever part of life we're struggling with. (Oh, you're losing your mind with your three-year-old? Me too!) These relationships will become strained from time to time. Tell me you never fight with your sister. I do. And I'm in my sixties. If

I don't always get along with my sister, what makes me think I will always get along with Darrell,[1] the obnoxious Patriots fan? I mean, who roots for the Patriots in Indiana?

But that's all a church is, really. Just a group of people trying to make it through whatever life throws at them while trying to keep a tight grip on the hand of Jesus. Doesn't need a 501(c)(3) designation from the IRS. Doesn't need a constitution and bylaws. Doesn't even need to get together once a week to sing three or four songs then listen to someone give a lecture about God stuff. It's just a group of people brought together by their mutual love for Jesus. Everything else can be stripped away, but if we lose this, we don't have a church any longer. We might still have an impressive show with fancy LED lights and smoke machines and incredible singers and an impressive speaker, but if we lose our identity as people joined together by their mutual love for God and desire to live like Jesus, a show is all we have.

I bring all this up because I think a lot of us are pretty much done with the light shows and smoke machines and hip speakers and whirlwinds of activities. We long for something more organic and less programmed, something that feels more like a family-owned Italian restaurant and less like an Olive Garden.[2] Deep down I think what we really want is the Jesus-based connection to others, and even that is difficult for us introverts.

I know it sounds like I am ragging on churches. I'm not. Nor am I saying that churches need to scrap all the programs and ministries and everything else that fills up the church schedule. Lives are indeed changed through these programs and ministries. I am the person I am today in part because of all the

---

1. Name changed in the hope that he will someday see the light. But you know who you are. Yeah, I'm talking about you!

2. This is in no way a put-down of my oldest granddaughter's favorite restaurant, the Olive Garden. Unlimited salad and breadsticks? Yes, please.

time I spent hanging out at youth events at Regency Park Baptist Church in Moore, Oklahoma, and the leadership of Troy McCoy, our youth director, who was older than my dad. I first started reading the Bible because of a Tuesday night group we called Read and Rap. Man, that was a cool name in 1975. We got together to read the Bible and rap about it. For those born after 1970, rap means to talk about in a cool, informal, totally groovy way. Far out, man. But I digress.

People love to rag on churches. My dad did. In every conversation we ever had, inevitably he'd utter these same seven words: "My problem with the organized church is . . ." Then he'd go off on some rant about one of the big churches in his area or some famous television preacher or whatever it was that was stuck in my dad's craw that particular day. My dad had a very sticky craw because stuff was always stuck in it. And nothing stuck in his craw like "the organized church." I always asked if he preferred a disorganized one. No matter how many times I said this to him, he always laughed. I should have been the one laughing, because what I never told him was that most churches aren't nearly as organized as they seem.

If you've spent much time behind the scenes in any church, the above should not surprise you. Let me tell you a little-known secret about churches and pastors: We're all just winging it. Not all of it, but a lot of it. Or at least some of it. I know I did. I called myself the king of wing for a reason. Not that I winged everything. When I was a pastor, I loved preaching, and not just the speaking part. I loved transporting myself to the ancient world through my Greek New Testament on Mondays and translating and making notes and even diagramming each verse phrase by phrase. Yes, I am a nerd when it comes to Bible study. Then I'd spend the rest of the week turning the passage of the week over and over in my mind and trying to figure out a way to make the passage come to life in a relatable way to my church. No winging it here.

Nor did I wing it on the deeply relational parts of the job. A lot of days I had no idea what I was supposed to do with myself beyond sermon prep, but when a crisis hit, I was in my element. Maybe it was the firefighter in me, but I loved sitting with people in hospital waiting rooms or walking with them through the worst days of their lives. The best day of my pastoral career was standing in a hospital ICU room with a woman whose husband had just come out of heart surgery. She looked at the tubes and wires and the beeping machines then turned to me and asked, "Pastor, what do I do?" I told her to take him by the hand and just be there with him. I don't know if that was the best advice in the world, but it helped her move past her fears and see her husband lying there, not just a collection of medical equipment fighting to keep him alive. She needed someone to give her that permission, and I had the honor of being the one. I miss these parts of my old career.

I don't miss the budget meetings. I don't miss the strategizing to figure out how to increase our market share, er, I mean, reach more people. I don't miss business meetings, because they reminded me of the unpleasant fact that I never wanted to admit to myself: A church is a business and I'm no entrepreneur. That part I had to wing. I had no choice because, like every other business, churches have overhead costs, personnel costs, and building acquisition and maintenance costs. We sing about heaven, but the bottom line is churches have to periodically spend a lot of money to repave the parking lot and replace the carpeting and change out light bulbs. But that's not the only way a church is a business.

Like any business, the church has to continually increase its customer base in order to be successful. "How's your church going?" one pastor will ask another, which simply means, "How many people do you have coming through the doors?" Customer acquisition and retention are high priorities, not that any pastor I know thinks of parishioners as customers. People are people, and in the words of Hieronymus Bosch,[3] everyone counts or no one counts. But to know who counts, we have to count, and the higher the count the better. That's the only real way pastors and churches have to measure whether or not they are successful in what they are doing.

*Whoa, hold on!* you're probably screaming at this book right now. Calling the Lord's house nothing more than a business is the kind of thinking that caused Jesus to start flipping over tables in the Temple. I do not disagree. *Our church is not a business*, many will protest, except the business of changing lives. Again, I am with you. This is the ideal.

However, the ideal is not reality, no matter how much we want to tell ourselves otherwise. And here's the reality: People who are looking for a church home may say they are praying for that place where God wants them, but the bottom line is they are consumers with an eye toward what any consumer wants. Comfort is big on the list. As are services, and not necessarily the worship kind, although those matter as well. If church shoppers have young children, they look for a church with the best children's programming. If they have teenagers, they look for the most vibrant teen programming. If they are old, they look for good senior programming. If they have ears, they look for a church with good music. If they have a normal human attention span, they look for a church with a dynamic pastor who will hold their attention. If they've ever been to a concert, they look for a church service that creates some of the same energy. If it

3. Michael Connelly's fictional detective, not the famous painter.

sounds like people choose churches based on something as crass as entertainment value, the truth is THEY DO! Let's get real, who wants to sit through something boring week after week? No one! That is why the Hillsong franchise churches grew so rapidly. The entire model was designed to create a user experience that made customers return week after week. It was the very definition of Church, Inc., shaped and driven by market forces.

The downside of serving churches in the Church, Inc., era, and every church and pastor at some point find themselves on the downside, is you consistently find yourself in a place where you lose people into whom you have poured your life as they feel God's call to go to a church down the road with a younger, more dynamic youth pastor or a stronger children's program or an overall better Sunday morning experience. To put it in business terms, you are losing customers. Every business thinks in terms of customer acquisition and retention, which is why McDonald's rolls out the McRib sandwich "for a limited time" every year and why Menards sells Shasta sodas along with building materials. You have to diversify and come up with new approaches to keep the business humming along. If you don't, your competitor will.

New approaches mean new ministries and new staff members. New staff members have new ideas and feel the need to create new and better programming as part of their calling to the church. New and better programming means more activities, creating the need for more volunteers and more space, which leads to more and more and more. Volunteers are always in short supply in every church, which means the leadership team must place a greater and greater emphasis on serving somewhere inside the church. With time the church becomes more and more building centric with a broader and broader schedule of events taking place there.

In the midst of it all, it's easy to lose sight of what the church really is in the whirlwind of activities we associate with what churches do.

But without the activities, people drift away to places that offer them. It's hard to be a group of people doing their best to love God and live like Jesus together without the group. For those tasked with leading these groups, nothing is as discouraging as watching your group wither away. Ministry isn't just some job we fell into when we had no better options coming out of college. For most people in full-time, or even part-time, ministry positions, this job is a calling. More than a calling, it becomes one's life. The pay often stinks (voice of experience talking); the hours can be wonky, especially when it comes to planning family trips; and the rewards can be frustrating.

Not that any of that matters.

When people heed the call to ministry, we don't just heed. We surrender to God to invest our lives in his people. When people do not respond in kind, we don't just feel frustrated. We feel defeated, as if we are failing the kingdom of God. How, then, can we tell if people have responded? By their attendance at Sunday services and then their attendance at a small group during the week and then their attendance at classes designed to go deeper into the Christian walk and then showing up to help with the kids or the teens or one of the many other ministries that needs committed people. The more they attend and volunteer, the greater the commitment, the more leaders lean on them. These are the success stories, the ones who have gone beyond attender to all in.

However, just as parishioners fall into a consumer mindset, leadership can do the same. Filling the activities with people becomes the unstated goal. As a result, the leadership team loses sight of how this group of people called a church are all just doing their best to love God and live like Jesus. Moreover, a disconnect often arises between the world inhabited by church leaders and parishioners. Of course pastors and church staff members face the same pressures as their parishioners. They feel the pressure of juggling work and home, of trying to be in three places at once when every child or grandchild in the family has a game or a match or a concert on the same night on opposite sides of town. Pastors shop at the same stores as their parishioners, and their children go to the same schools and play on the same teams and experience many of the same experiences.

Yet, and again, this is the voice of experience talking, anyone who serves a church vocationally does not inhabit the same world as those who work any other type of job. There is a detachment, a form of myopia that comes from not working day after day on a warehouse floor with people who regularly push you to your limits. Showing up at a midweek event at the church takes far less grip on the hand of Jesus than simply holding your tongue with a coworker you can barely keep from punching in the nose.

In the last chapter I wrote that sometimes I wonder if I go to church each week more out of habit than anything else. I hate to admit that I was not exaggerating. From conversations I have had over the past year or so, I also know I am not alone. The reason goes back to what my dad was ranting about all those years. It's not the organized church that gives me pause but Church, Inc., the church as a business, the church as an entertainment product, the church as a full-service stop for all of your spiritual needs. What I really want, what I think we all really want, is simply to connect with some other people doing their best to love God and live like Jesus. That's all a church really is, whether it is in Boston or Indianapolis or Los Angeles or ancient Ephesus in Asia Minor. We cannot allow ourselves to lose sight of this in a sea of activities put together in hopes of making such connections happen.

## A Final Word, Especially to Pastors

Yes, I have studied ecclesiology, and I know both theologically and historically that defining the church as a group of people who love God and are trying to live like Jesus together is a very, very limited definition.

No, I did not explain the role of the church in the ordinances of the church or, if you prefer, the sacraments. In no way does this omission lessen their importance.

Nor did I bring up the difference between the Church with a big C, i.e., the universal church that spreads across both time and space, and the church with a little *c*, i.e., the local expressions of the universal church, aka the local church. This chapter was never meant to be a comprehensive discussion of the Church or the church.

I also realize that I did not talk about the role of the church in celebrating the presence of God together in corporate worship. You may well have thought that I was downplaying or outright dismissing the need for corporate worship. That was not at all my intention.

I also was not downplaying or outright dismissing the role of full- or part-time professional pastors and staff. I have lived that life, and I know how absolutely difficult your job is, and I might well have reacted very negatively to a chapter like this thirty years ago.

But I didn't write this chapter thirty years ago when I was in the middle of performing spiritual CPR on a church that didn't realize it was nearly dead. I wrote it when I am in my sixties, looking back at both my career and my experiences in churches stretching back to the First Baptist Church of Altus, Oklahoma. I don't really remember that church since I was a week old when I started attending. Since then I have continuously been a member or in a primary leadership position in churches across the United States. My goal in writing this chapter was not to pile on to the endless voices of critics but to voice the heart cry I hear not only from deep inside myself but from family and friends who struggle to distinguish between the highly programmed model of church that has grown out of the rise of megachurches and their longing for real, organic connections with other believers.

This chapter also rose out of observing a nonprofit that works with women in the sex industry, primarily strip club dancers. One of my daughters started this nonprofit in her living room with a budget of $100 a year after graduating from college. Just under fifteen years later, she now has four full-time employees including herself and has impacted hundreds of lives in a very, very relational way. A couple of days ago my daughter told me that after spending her morning working on grant applications, she walked to the living room of her office to ask the program director a question, thinking a support group for their clients had ended two hours earlier. When my daughter walked into the room, half the women from the group were still there. "Oh hey, we're just having family time," one of the participants said. There's a biblical word for that "family time": Church.

Big C or little c, this relational connection between people who love God and are doing their best to follow Jesus together in the midst of a very difficult world is the heart of what makes a church a church. It's not the only element of ecclesiology, but without it all you have are the titles and the functions and not the Bride of Christ in all her beauty.

## NINE

# Can I Claim Jeremiah 29:11 as My Life Verse If I've Never Read the Book of Jeremiah?

I sometimes wonder what might have happened if the writers of Scripture lived in our world of social media and viral videos and influencers influencing whomever they actually influence. The question led me to imagine a conversation between a promotional agent and the Old Testament prophet Jeremiah and the apostle Paul. Perhaps it may have gone a little like this:

"Jerry, baby, step on into my office. We need to have a little sit-down, a come-to-Jesus meeting, if you will."

"Come to who?"

"Yeah, yeah, yeah, I keep forgetting. The Big Guy is after your time. You live in, what, 600 BC?"

"What's BC?"

"Never mind, never mind. Doesn't matter. What matters is this here book you've written."

"God spoke and I wrote."

"Sure, whatever, but it's your name that's on the top of it. Great big letters, J-E-R-E-M-I-A-H, correct?"

"I did not give it that title."

"But you wrote it, right? It's your words, your book. And I gotta tell you, as your agent, this book, it's, uh, well, I'm just going to come out and give it to you straight, it's a downer. Major, major downer."

"What did you expect? I wrote it during the darkest days of Judah's history. The northern kingdom had already fallen. Now it was our turn. When my home city of Jerusalem was surrounded and people were starving to death, light and fluffy wasn't exactly in order. Have you read my other book, Lamentations?"

"Uh, no. It sounds like a real page-turner, but let's get back to your first book. Why does it have to be so depressing? You wrote right here in chapter nine . . ."

"Chapter?"

"Oh yeah. I forgot to tell you. A couple thousand years after you wrote the book, someone came along and divided it all up into chapters and verses."

"Verses?"

"Jerry, baby, doesn't matter. What matters is what you wrote right here in chapter nine, verse one, and I quote, 'Oh, that my head were a spring of water and my eyes a fountain of tears! I would weep day and night for the slain of my people.'[1] Really, Jer, weeping day and night? I gotta be straight with ya and tell ya that most people, and market research bears me out on this, most people are not going to keep reading when you start talking about weeping over the slain of your people. People read

1. NIV.

the Bible to feel happy. They want something that's going to make them feel better about their lives."

"But the people to whom I wrote this had forsaken the Lord. God gave them innumerable chances over hundreds of years to turn back to him, but they never did. That's why he sent the Babylonian army to destroy the entire country. It was divine judgment. People died every day. It's what was happening. I don't care if people find this to be a downer, whatever that word means. The point of writing all this down was so that future generations would learn from our mistakes and not forsake the Lord Almighty."

"Big J, buddy, preaching to the choir, okay. I get it. But people . . . people want what they want, and more than anything else, they want to be uplifted. They want to be inspired. They want something they can claim as their own, something that gives them hope."

"But there is hope in what I wrote. The entire book is brimming with hope. After the time of judgment is over, he will bring the people back to the promised land, where they will be his people and he will be their God. Eventually he will even send the Messiah to save them once and for all."

"Hey, I thought you didn't know about Jesus."

"Who?"

"Never mind. You're in for a very pleasant surprise. But let's get back to this hope. Where exactly in this depressing little tome of yours will I find these messages of hope?"

"Near the middle, just a little before the midpoint of the book in a letter I wrote to the exiles in Babylon. You see, false prophets were telling the people that the Lord was going to bring everyone who had been carried away to Babylon back home within a year or two."

"I don't mean to interrupt, but what are you talking about with these exiles?"

"Haven't you read my book?"

"Well, not all of it, but most of it. At least part of it. I mean, I skimmed it."

"And you're my agent?"

"Listen, J Dog, I don't have to read the whole thing to represent you well."

"How did I end up with you as my agent, anyways?"

"No idea. But since I am, will you explain this whole exile thing to me?"

"In my time, which I guess to you is the ancient world, when one country conquered another, they carried off the best of everything they could find as the spoils of war. You know, to the victors go the spoils. In our case, the Babylonian army under King Nebuchadnezzar took all the gold, silver, and precious stones they could carry. They also took away the best and the brightest people to serve them. Those people, the ones carried away as slaves to Babylon, those are the exiles."

"Best and brightest? And you didn't make the cut, huh?"

"I chose to stay behind. This is the place where God called me to be his spokesperson, his prophet, to speak his word to his people as judgment happened so that they would know these were not some random events."

"Again with the downers, and nothing is a bigger downer than judgment. Ugh. You said there was hope in here somewhere. You need to get to it and quick."

"The hope is in the letter to the exiles. I told them to settle in because they were going to be in Babylon for a long time, seventy years in total. But then God was going to bring them back. God also gave me a special word for them. He told me to tell them, "'For I know the plans I have for you,'" says the Lord. "They are plans for good and not for disaster, to give you a future and a hope."'"[2]

"Wait a minute! Could you repeat that for me?"

"For I know the plans I have for you. They are plans for good and not for disaster, to give you a future and a hope."

"Boom, baby!! That's it, Jeremiah, my man! Now that's a verse I can do things with. Plans for good and not for disaster. To give you a future and a hope. Look at my arms. What do you see? Chills, that's what. I can see it now. We can plaster this on coffee mugs and T-shirts and print it in some fancy font and have people put it up on the walls in their homes. Jerry, baby, I'm telling you, this is gold. GOLD, I'm telling ya!"

"Did you not hear the part about seventy years in exile?"

"Exile, schmexile. Doesn't matter. All that matters is this is one of those verses people can latch on to. Going through something bad? Just reach for this verse. You're a genius, Jeremiah. A literary genius."

"But if people don't read the rest of the book and don't understand the context, won't they use this verse in ways I never intended? Forget about me because these aren't my words. God spoke them. He just used me to put them down on parchment. Part of the reason judgment came in my day was because of the way his people did not keep his word but instead twisted it to say whatever it was they wanted to hear. Can you not see the same danger here?"

"There's nothing to worry about, my man. You write it and leave the marketing to me."

"I don't know what marketing even is, but if people don't read the rest of the book, they'll never understand this verse.

2. Jeremiah 29:11.

It's not some pithy little saying to repeat to yourself when you're feeling down. These words were written to a people who had once been close to God but had turned their backs on him for generations. God was doing whatever was necessary to bring them back to him, even if it meant all of their nightmares were coming true and were going to keep coming true for longer than most of them were going to live. But that didn't mean God's plan for them had passed. He still had a plan for his people. In spite of the judgment, he still had a future and a hope for them. Even if the people first reading this didn't live to see it, God's plan was still at work, even with the pain."

"I'm sorry, I wasn't listening. Listen, Jerry, you've got a good thing here, so let's not spoil it, okay? I really enjoyed our little talk but, whew, look at the time, I've got another client waiting for me. I'll be in touch."

"But . . ."

"I'll see you later. My next client is . . . hey, look at this. He's already here. Paul, Pauly, my man, the apostle to the gentiles himself in the flesh, so good of you to drop by. And I've got to tell you, Pauly baby, I am absolutely loving these letters of yours. *Loving* them! In fact, I love them so much I think we need to do a little something to give them a bit more gravitas, if you know what I mean."

"I have absolutely no idea what you are talking about."

"Gravitas, you know, a little more of that 'it' factor that lets people know they better read this stuff because it is lit."

"Lit?"

"You know, powerful. And they need a powerful name to get this across, so I'm thinking that instead of calling them letters, we should call them—are you sitting down, oh, of course you are—let's call them epistles."

"Isn't that just another word for letters?"

"You know that, and I know that, but the people out there, not all of them realize that, and even if they do, *epistles* sounds like a smart word that smart people will use, and people like to feel smart, especially when reading the Bible."

"But God has made the wisdom of this world look foolish."

"First Corinthians chapter one! Boom. I told you I love your letters, er, epistles. The words, they just roll right off the page. And I gotta tell you, of all the letters you've written, the one to the church in Philippians has got to be my favorite."

"Philippi."

"Excuse me?"

"Philippi was the city. The people who lived there were called Philippians."

"Tomato, tomahto, I'm just saying this letter, it speaks to me."

"That's the prayer—that every Christ follower's heart will be open to hear the Word of the Lord."

"Mine is open and has received it with a big ole hug. You touched me, right here, especially the last chapter."

"The last what?"

"I keep forgetting you guys who wrote the Bible weren't the ones who divided it into chapters and verses. That came much later, which is a good thing because it makes it possible for people like me to just say the reference, and people will get what we're saying. For me, that is Philippians 4:13."

"Which sentence are you referring to specifically?"

"4:13. I can do everything through Christ who gives me strength."

"And the rest of the paragraph?"

"What about it?"

"The sentence you just quoted. It's part of an entire paragraph where I express my thanks to the church in Philippi for their concern and support for me. Not that I was ever in need, for I learned how to be content with whatever I have. Whether I have nothing or everything, a full stomach or empty, it doesn't matter. Whatever difficulties I face as I live out my mission for God, I can do everything through Christ who gives me strength."[3]

"That's beautiful, man. So here's what I'm thinking of doing with it. I am going to run a 5K race this weekend, working my way up to do a marathon . . ."

"I've been there. Beautiful village, Marathonos. So many olive trees where a huge battle once raged."

"Anyway, I plan on putting Philippians 4:13 on a T-shirt and wearing it while I run and maybe even writing the words Philippians 4:13 down my leg with a Sharpie so that people get the message that I can run this 5K through Christ who gives me strength. I mean, other athletes do it. I've seen them write it on their sneakers when they play basketball and on their baseball mitt in a big game. This verse of yours, it's pretty much the theme verse for every Christian athlete and everyone else who attempts something difficult. I heard of one team of Christian mountain climbers who used this as their theme verse when they climbed Mount Everest."

"I didn't really understand half of what you were saying, but let me be clear, these words do not mean that Jesus is going to give you extra power so that you can run some sort of race."

"I beg to disagree, Mr. Apostle Paul. Didn't you write, and I quote, 'Don't you realize that in a race everyone runs, but only one person gets the prize? So run to win!'"[4]

3. Paraphrase of Philippians 4:10–14.
4. 1 Corinthians 9:24.

"I wasn't talking about a literal race. I used athletic training as an analogy for how I discipline myself to stay true to Jesus and his calling on my life. And that's what I was talking about in my letter to the Philippians. The sentence you quoted does not mean that God will give you an extra energy boost to run a long distance or compete in any of these strange-sounding sports you've mentioned. These words are meant to be an encouragement to other Christ followers that whatever situation God calls you into, he will give you the strength to live out your love for Jesus in it. It doesn't matter if you have everything you could ever desire or if you have nothing at all. God is faithful, and he will give you the power to stay faithful to him through it. You are taking my words completely out of context!"

"Whoa, whoa, whoa, big fella. Didn't mean to get you all stirred up. All I'm saying is your words are an inspiration to millions. And if a few of us quote this masterpiece of a line to give ourselves a little boost before we, I don't know, step up to bat with the bases loaded in the bottom of the ninth of the World Series, is that so wrong?"

"I have no idea what bats and bases and bottoms of ninths are, but I understand enough from your context to tell you that you are getting very close to turning the words the Holy Spirit moved me to write into nothing more than an inspirational saying that doesn't have any real meaning. You know, back in my day, there was this guy in Rome whose cat fell out of a window but saved itself when it caught hold of a clothesline. I don't know if you still have those, but back then people hung their clothes on ropes strung between buildings to dry after washing. Anyway, this cat grabbed hold of the clothesline, and my friend said 'Hang in there' to his cat. I don't see much difference between what you're doing by writing Philippians 4:13 on your leg and what my friend said to his cat."

"I love that cat line. Do you mind if I put that on a poster? I think it will sell."

"Are you serious?"

"So Philippians 4:13 isn't the only verse I wanted to talk to you about. The other is, and I love this one so much, Romans 8:28."

"I'm sorry. I do not know what these numbers refer to. Can you be more specific, please?"

"And we know that God causes everything to work together for the good of those who love God and are called according to his purpose for them."

"Okay. Yes. I placed that sentence in the middle of a discussion of the future glory God has in store for us in light of the suffering we face in this world."

"Yeah, yeah, yeah, that's great, but what I really love about this verse is the promise from God that tells us that everything happens for a reason and God will make everything turn out okay for us."

"Wait. What?"

"When I experience anything negative, I can be assured that God is going to spin it around for a positive. Reminds me of that line from Genesis where Joseph told his brothers that what they intended for evil, God intended for good.[5] That's what your verse tells me. Satan tries to hit me with evil, but God will turn it all around for good. God's got a plan, and that plan is for good, not evil. My other client, Jeremiah, he basically wrote the same thing. Great guy. You ought to get to know him."

"I think you misunderstood the scope of what I was saying. Yes, God does cause everything to work together for the good of those who love him and are called to his purpose for them. But I

5. Genesis 50:20.

then go on to explain how this works in the big picture of God's plan for his children that stretches out past this life. Jesus himself said that in this life we will have trouble, but we can take heart because he overcame the world.[6] He overcame the world when he died on the cross and rose again on the third day. That's the heart of what I wrote in the entirety of the passage you quoted. God did not spare his own Son for us, and he promises us that he will give us everything else he has promised his children. My point in writing all of this is to reassure Christ followers that even if we go through calamity and persecution and hunger or become destitute or experience every other horrible thing this world can throw at us, God's love remains constant and his plan for us cannot be stopped.[7] His plan started long before any of us were ever born. He knew his people in advance and chose them to become like Jesus. He not only chose us but he called us to himself. For me, that call came on the road to Damascus. After he calls us, he justifies us. That is, he gives us right standing with him and adopts us into his family. And everyone he justifies, he also glorifies. We don't see the latter in this life, but we will enjoy it for all eternity in his presence.[8] That's the good I'm talking about in what you have labeled Romans 8:28. It's a big-picture promise of the work God does in our lives, not some sort of guarantee that he's going to rescue us from everything bad that ever happens. This promise doesn't even mean that everything happens for some divine reason. God didn't tell that crowd in Lystra to pick up rocks and try to stone me to death. They came up with that plan on their own without divine instructions. I can still feel those rocks."

"I'm sorry. I sort of dozed off there in the middle of your sermon, but if I heard you correctly, you're telling me, and I can't

6. John 16:33.
7. Romans 8:31–39.
8. Romans 8:28–30.

believe this is even possible, that every bad thing that happens to me won't be turned into something good?"

"Ultimately it will, but not in this life. But of course, this life is just a vapor. Would you rather have a string of happy endings in the brevity of this life or in eternity?"

"Will you hate me if I say both?"

"No, I'd say that makes you human. But you have to remember, these promises come as a package deal. They're not a means for you to escape the realities of living in a broken, sinful, fallen world. Instead, God gives us these promises so that despite all the bad we face, overwhelming victory is ours through Christ who loves us."[9]

"I still want both."

"We all do. Do you honestly think I enjoy getting beaten up by angry crowds or enduring a shipwreck or spending years in prison? But you know that letter you said you love so much, the one I wrote to the church in Philippi? I wrote that one from jail."

"But it's so positive. I never would have guessed you were in prison when you wrote it."

"Isn't that the point? Enduring prison after being thrown in jail for preaching Jesus, those are all things I can do through Christ who gives me strength."

"So these promises you wrote about . . ."

"That God gave me. I didn't come up with them on my own."

"Sure, that God gave you. They, uh, how do I say this, they aren't about me as much as they are about God?"

"They are for you, but yes, they are about God and his faithfulness and how he works in and through his children to put his power and love on display for the whole world to see."[10]

9. Romans 8:37.
10. Ephesians 3:10.

"That's harder to put on a T-shirt."

"A what?"

## A Final Word to Those Who Claim These Verses and Others as Their Favorites

I love Jeremiah 29:11, Philippians 4:13, and Romans 8:28 as much as any of you. This chapter in no way implies that you cannot claim them as life verses. However, no passage of Scripture exists in a vacuum. The writers of the Bible did not set out to pen inspirational sayings. They wrote the very Word of God as moved by the Holy Spirit. Every verse in the Bible is part of a larger context, beginning with the verses around it, then with the chapter in which it is found, then within the book as a whole, and finally within the context of the entire Bible, both Old and New Testaments. Removing a verse from its context, no matter how inspiring you may find it, is a misuse of Scripture. I don't like it when someone takes my words out of context, which is perhaps a line I should have included in the chapter about parenting. I doubt if you care for having your words taken out of context, either. Imagine, then, how God must feel. However, there is good news in the midst of this warning. When you meditate upon a verse within its larger context, you will experience a deeper understanding of both the passage and of God. This is the place where real life change takes place.

## TEN

# What If I'm Wrong?

When I first started working on this book, I could not wait to get to this chapter. I was so excited about it that at one point I rearranged the table of contents to make this the first chapter rather than the last. About three-quarters of the way through writing my first attempt of this chapter, I realized that my original first chapter needed to kick off the book and this one needed to bookend it as the last. However, my efforts were not a total waste of time. Much of that first draft of this chapter became the introduction of the book.

I write this little story not so much as a way of introducing this chapter but as more of a delay tactic because, in all honesty, I don't want to ask myself this question. I was quite excited about asking you to wrestle with it, but for me personally, not so much. I did not mind taking you on a journey of self-discovery or forcing you to come face-to-face with the possibility of being wrong about whatever you may hold to be certain. My enthusiasm waned when I posed the question to myself. The question I have to address is not "What if *you* are wrong?" but "What if *I* am wrong?" I can't expect anyone to take this chapter or even this book seriously if I am not willing to ask myself this question.

And that's the kicker. We can all easily see where *you* (that is, the ubiquitous "they") have specks of dust in their eyes in spite of the planks we carry around in our own eyes. Those who love pineapple on pizza know all pineapple haters are dead wrong, and the pineapple haters believe putting any fruit on pizza is a mortal sin. Red Sox fans know how wrong Yankees fans are, and Yankees fans feel the same way about everyone who doesn't live and die for the pinstripes. "They're wrong" flows easily from my lips, but to stop and ask myself "What if *I* am wrong?" forces me to admit that I am the smug one who needs to dig deep inside myself. I am the one who doesn't have life nearly as figured out as I like to tell myself. Ecclesiastes 7:14 says that nothing in this life is certain, but I pretend otherwise. I surround myself with an imaginary wall of certainties only to watch it fall apart on a daily basis. I prefer to keep my eyes closed, but the title question forces me to open them up and see the truth I can't handle.

I guess what I am really saying is I prefer we all skip this chapter and go off on our happy way of living in all the certainties with which we surround ourselves. Instead of a chapter called "What If I Am Wrong?" how about a chapter called "What Am I So Afraid Of?" or "Does It Really Matter?" or "Do I Treat God Like an Algorithm?" all of which I have worked on as alternatives to this chapter. But no matter how hard I pushed, "What If I Am Wrong?" refused to surrender its place in this book. I guess I now have to ask myself the question I don't think any of us want to ask ourselves: What if I am wrong?

*Wrong about what?* you ask. Here's the hard part; here's what makes this a question I want to avoid but cannot: What if I am wrong . . . about everything! I don't know about you, but dramatic music just played in my head. Oh boy. This is going to be a *lot* of fun. Sarcasm intended.

## Let's Start Easy

I don't want to dig too deep too quickly. I don't know that I can handle that. Instead, I think I'll start off with something easy like . . . what if I am wrong about the breakfast choice I just made? While writing this chapter, I took a long break between sections to gather my thoughts, but really, it was to get away from asking questions I don't want to ask. During this break I ate my usual breakfast of oatmeal with a glass of grape juice. I used to drink orange juice, but it started causing me to have acid reflux because I am over sixty, so I switched to grape juice and good grief this is boring but that's what I want. I prefer boring and easy over diving into the questions lurking below, so here are some even more boring details about my breakfast. I added walnuts and a touch of maple syrup to the oatmeal and it waaaaaaaaa.

Sorry, I dozed off there for a moment on the "a" key. I'm back now and am ready to ask the hard-hitting question on everyone's mind: What if I am wrong about my breakfast choice? If you are following along at home, feel free to ask yourselves this same hard-hitting question.

I've brought back Past, Present, and Future Me as our panel of experts who will judge these questions on a three-point scale: Relevance, Relatability, and Real World Consequences. They are not here to answer the question of whether or not I am wrong. That's not the question of the day. The question is, Should I explore this area of my life deeper? And the judges say:

1. Relevance: No one cares.
2. Relatability: Again, no one cares.
3. Real World Consequences: You're kidding, right?

That was painless enough. Perhaps I will venture into a little harder question that I have done my best to avoid asking myself. Here goes. Deep breath. I'm not sure I am ready to discover what I might find here. The next question is, What if I am wrong and the dachshund is not the pinnacle of dog evolution? After all, a doxie has never won the prestigious Westminster Dog Show. Dachshunds are also stubborn and difficult to train. They have no respect for a human being's personal space. Even if you are one of those strange humans who does not love dogs, a dachshund will jump on your lap and insist you give your undivided attention to her. They bark a lot and sleep twenty-three hours a day and show absolutely zero signs of being a dog first bred to crawl deep underground and drag an angry badger out of its den. However, in spite of their flaws, if you have ever had one, you cannot help but think it is the greatest dog breed in the world. But what if I am wrong? What do the judges say?

1. Relevance: A dog lover might find this question slightly interesting. Cat lovers quit reading this chapter a long time ago.

2. Relatability: Every dog lover believes their favorite breed should be everyone's favorite breed. In their own eyes, they are right. Except doodle owners. Why are there so many doodles?

3. Real World Consequences: Aside from the possibility of a playground scuffle over this question between two ten-year-old boys who don't need a reason to scuffle, it's hard to imagine any real world consequences from this question, although dog show judges should have to answer the question of why a dachshund has never won best in show.

Whew. Outside of a couple of deep breaths, I came through that examination of a key part of my belief system relatively unscathed. Now the question is, Do I dare go deeper? I do not want to. I'd rather fiddle around with trivial matters than dive into one area I'm not even sure I should explore. To do so invites doubt, and doubt is the opposite of what this area of my life demands. It demands faith. And faith means certainty. Rock-solid certainty based on solid evidence that demands a verdict. And the only verdict that can be rendered is belief. This is true beyond a shadow of a doubt. How could I be wrong? But what if I am? What if I am wrong about God?

I think my three judges ran out of the room rather than deal with this question.

## Is This Something We Should Even Ask?

Of all the questions in this book, none has drawn more concerned looks from friends than this one. People don't just look at me like I've lost my mind, although they fear I have. They give me an alarmed look like I have lost something far more valuable, i.e., my faith. Asking if I am wrong about God appears to say that I have abandoned everything I once held dear and have crossed the line from believer to skeptic, from faithful to faithless, from Christ follower to agnostic. Let me assure you that nothing could be further from the truth.

What if I am wrong about God is not a statement of doubt. I do not doubt God's existence, nor do I doubt the Bible. I have complete confidence that Jesus was born of a virgin, lived a sinless life, died on a cross for the sins of the world past, present, and future, and rose again on the third day. I believe Jesus will return someday just as he promised before he ascended into heaven. Not only do I believe all of the above but I have staked my life on it. I am all in with no turning back.

However, the uncomfortable truth about all I believe, and about what you believe as well, whether you believe in the historicity of the Bible or think it's all a fairy tale, is that neither of us has absolute proof. We may be certain and think the other side is made up of fools, but that doesn't change the fact that our "proofs and truths" are very much in the eye of the beholder. I cannot speak about this effectively on the nonbelieving side since I crossed that line as a child and reaffirmed it at the cusp of full adulthood. But I can speak of this from the believer's side, and if I am honest, I must admit that I have no absolute proof for the things I believe.

Now before you run and grab a bucket of tar and a bag of feathers, please hear me out. Hebrews 11:1 says "Faith shows the reality of what we hope for; it is the evidence of things we cannot see." What we hope for and what we cannot see do not produce proof that leads me to believe. Rather, it is faith itself that produces the reality of what I hope for and gives me the evidence of what I cannot see. Or, as I believe someone said in the movie *The Santa Clause*, seeing is not believing; believing is seeing. The line may have come from a movie about Santa Claus, but that fact does not make it any less true.

Our beliefs shape how we perceive everything else, no matter what we believe. It is why King David could look up at the sky and declare, "The heavens proclaim the glory of God. The skies display his craftsmanship,"[1] while Russian cosmonaut Gherman Titov, the second man to fly into space, declared during his flight aboard a Vostok rocket, "Some say God is living there [in space]. I was looking around very attentively, but I did not see

1. Psalm 19:1.

anyone there."[2] David saw the hand of God and Titov saw an empty void in large part because that's what they were looking for. *But Titov misunderstood how God shows himself*, we might protest. Titov would probably say the same of David.

I look at the complexity of life on earth and how the planet seems fine-tuned for it as evidence of the Creator. I've read the works of physicists who see this same fine-tuning as evidence of the existence of the multiverse, filled with universes, both those that support life and those that do not. The fact that we live in a universe that supports life is, according to those who ascribe to that theory, a happy accident, not proof of a creator. Obviously, both of us cannot be correct, and I am convinced that I am. However, it is a fine line to go from convinced of my rightness to mistaking my certainty about God for intellectual superiority. In other words, when we are absolutely convinced that we know the truth and that there is no way we can be wrong, we end up thinking we are smarter than everyone else in the room, something I unfortunately have a lot of experience with. Ironically, when we take on such a posture in our beliefs about God, we place ourselves in a position of opposition to him. I know that sounds absolutely bonkers, but hear me out.

James 4:6 states, "God opposes the proud but gives grace to the humble." As I wrote earlier, I remind myself of this verse every single day. Pride is offensive to God. It is the very essence of the original sin from the garden of Eden. Pride motivated the first man and woman to take hold of the fruit that could possibly make them like God. Something inside every one of their descendants makes us hate being looked down upon. We prefer to do the looking down ourselves, an urge that does not

2. Christine Spillson, "Lower Orbits: Remembering Gherman Titov," *The Rumpus*, August 3, 2017, https://therumpus.net/2017/08/03/lower-orbits-remembering-gherman-titov/.

automatically go away when we cross the line from unbelief to Christ follower. And nothing is more disgusting than taking on an air that I made this journey fully on my own, as if I figured out the truth that should be so obvious to everyone. Anyone who can't see this truth, well, they are obviously idiots.

Therefore, asking ourselves the question, What if I am wrong?, especially about God, is not an entryway into the world of doubt but a call to humility. Faith in Jesus is not the mark of a superior intellect. In fact, Paul wrote in the first chapter of 1 Corinthians that God purposefully did not call those the world considers wise to believe, nor the powerful nor the wealthy. God shows his power by calling outcasts. That doesn't mean all Christ followers are subpar intellectually but rather that the truth about Jesus is lost on all of us who try to grasp it from a purely human level. Paul put it this way:

> Since God in his wisdom saw to it that the world would never know him through human wisdom, he has used our foolish preaching to save those who believe. It is foolish to the Jews, who ask for signs from heaven. And it is foolish to the Greeks, who seek human wisdom. So when we preach that Christ was crucified, the Jews are offended and the Gentiles say it's all nonsense. But to those called by God to salvation, both Jews and Gentiles, Christ is the power of God and the wisdom of God.[3]

Again, my purpose with these questions is not to create doubt. Rather, the very thought that my entire belief system could be wrong should lead me daily to a place of humility in my interactions with people and in my walk with God. The Christian life is lived by faith rooted in grace. We are saved by

3. 1 Corinthians 1:21–24.

grace. Even believing is a gift of God's grace. If not for God's grace, every believer would be an unbeliever and the truths that seem so certain would sound like pure foolishness. Grace cannot be received by the proud, because the proud can never wrap their heads around something so absurd.

## Only the Beginning

The proud also have difficulty honestly asking themselves the title question. Proud or not, no one wants to be wrong. No one celebrates on *Jeopardy!* when they go all in on the Daily Double then give a wrong answer, er, question since we're talking about *Jeopardy!* Parents don't take kids out for ice cream for failing a history test, just as no one wants to be Neville Chamberlain and end up on the wrong side of history. Everyone wants to be Sherlock Holmes, who solves the mystery, not the bumbling police detective, who jumped to a very wrong conclusion. Might is right and right is might but wrong is just wrong and no one wants to go there. Being proven wrong is one of our greatest fears.

And this is what makes this chapter so important to me. Christ followers are called to walk humbly with our God. Micah 6:8 calls it one of the three things God requires of us, along with acting justly and loving mercy. The opposite of humility is not just pride. It is the refusal to even consider the possibility of being wrong. Obviously, only a sociopath claims they are never wrong. But the fear of being wrong and the refusal to even consider it shows up in far more subtle and destructive ways in most of our lives. It manifests itself in the insatiable desire to always be in control. We may joke about being a control freak, but it is no laughing matter. If I have to be in control of every situation, I am in effect telling everyone around me that I am right and you are wrong and the only right course is to let me be in charge. But what if I am wrong?

The refusal to consider that I might be wrong also comes out in arrogance and overconfidence. I'm no psychologist, but I have worked with people for a very long time. I have found, both in myself and in others, that people are often the most outspoken and demanding to have their voice prevail in questions where a shadow of a doubt keeps popping up in their brain. Shouting down all other voices is often simply our way of trying to silence the voice of doubt within ourselves. Perhaps we need to listen instead.

Finally, I believe the most insidious and dangerous way in which our refusal to even think that we might be wrong shows up is in our surrounding ourselves with people and voices that reaffirm all that we already believe. Some call it a silo. I call it a box. God doesn't fit into boxes, but that doesn't stop us from trying to cram him into one as well as everything else in our lives. We fill the box with talk radio and blogs and social media friends who already think like us and see the world like us. Before long we begin to believe that ours is the only way, the only truth, the only way to navigate life. Anyone who sees the world in a different way we keep at arm's length at best or at worst consider an enemy to be silenced.

But what if we are wrong? What if all the people and voices in our little box are wrong as well? We don't have to be wrong about everything, or even most things, to place ourselves in a precarious place. The apostle Paul said even a little yeast leavens the whole loaf. Opening myself to the possibility of being corrected and learning a new truth keeps the leaven at bay.

"What if I am wrong?" is less an actual question I ask myself than it is an attitude of always being open to learning new things and always being ready to adjust my course. The fictional soccer coach Ted Lasso captured the essence of this attitude when he said, "Be curious, not judgmental."[4] Curiosity dies when we assume we have life all figured out, that we know all the answers without even asking the questions, that we are right and you are wrong. That's no way to live. I prefer to live by faith in the living God who calls me to trust him in a world of uncertainty. Yes, I may be wrong, but I believe I am not, at least not about God, which is the very definition of faith. You cannot have faith without uncertainty, and you cannot have uncertainty if you never ask yourself, But what if I am wrong? This is the question that ultimately led to the book you just finished. I hope the questions do not end when you close the cover.

## A Final Word for Every Reader

There's a reason this chapter had to be last. Years ago, long before I ever wondered if I might be a better Christian on Zoloft, I found myself wrestling with an uneasiness that had come over me. At first I thought it might be boredom, since I had not gone off on some crazy adventure of faith since my wife and I adopted our two youngest daughters. It wasn't boredom. Then I explored the question that eventually became chapter 7, "Why Don't I Feel It?" I wondered if the uneasiness I felt was some sort of residual effects of spiritual burnout, like a burned-over field after an Oklahoma grass fire. But I wasn't spiritually burned out. I simply wasn't feeling it, but then again, I'd gone through times of not feeling it going back to my early twenties.

4. *Ted Lasso*, "The Diamond Dogs," directed by Declan Lowney (Apple TV, September 20, 2020).

I find it is always a healthy experience when God weans me off of emotional lifts and forces me to trust him by faith alone. This uneasiness was more than that.

As you have probably guessed, the uneasiness was somehow related to this chapter's title question. In spite of all I had written in the past, both under my own name and in books I wrote with others about how nothing in this life is certain, I had slipped into a mindset where I had certain expectations for this stage of my life, and when those expectations did not come to pass, I struggled. Tomorrow was now today, and it had not turned out the way that I had expected, the way that I subconsciously had counted on it turning out all of my life. The uneasiness within me was really a longing for a certainty that does not exist. As this truth slowly began to dawn on me, it turned into a question I now ask myself daily. What if I am wrong? The question has been liberating.

All of us want certainty. We want to be certain our car will start in the morning and the computer will boot up when it is time to start work. We want the temperature in the house to go up when we crank up the thermostat in January and go down when we crank it down in July. We have people we count on and places we depend on. Certainty is what makes it possible to go about a normal life.

We also want certainty when it comes to God. That desire for certainty not only moves us to dismiss anyone who denies God but also to put God in a box of our expectations of him. I never believed I thought of God in this way . . . until my children became adults, but you probably guessed that after reading chapter 4. Many Christian parents of adult children can probably relate. We trained up that child in the way they should go. Why didn't God keep them from departing from it?

But parenthood is not the only way in which certainty can become a barrier in our relationship with God. Certainty corrupts faith, making it a means to an end rather than an end in itself, a way to get God to act on our behalf rather than simply believing God. I am convinced that many of the trials we experience in the Christian life are less a failure on God's part to act in a consistent manner and more an error on our part of misunderstanding who God is. We expect what he did not promise and are devastated when he doesn't follow through.

And this plays out every day in our lives. We beg God for healing, but death comes anyway. *I thought "by his stripes we are healed!"* we howl in protest, forgetting the fact that the death rate is now and has always been 100 percent. We claim the second half of Matthew 6:33 as a promise that "[God] will give you everything you need," when an unexpected bill shows up, while forgetting the first half, "Seek the Kingdom of God above all else and live righteously." We want a world where the good guys always win and the wicked always get what's coming to them, as if the script for life was written by the same guys who wrote *Walker, Texas Ranger*. That world does not exist outside of old TV reruns.

What if I am wrong is a lens through which to see the world where uncertainty reigns. It is a world filled with far more questions than answers. I hope this never changes. When I stop asking questions is when I stop learning, because learning always begins with a question, which is followed by a search for an answer. The day I stop learning is the day I stop living, even if my physical existence drags on. This is the road less certain, which is also the road of faith. It's a narrow road. Not a lot of travelers bother looking for it. It's a road with very few markers or signs. But it is the road that leads to life, not somewhere out there far away, but right now, in the middle of the journey itself.

# AFTERWORD

The original idea for this book came sort of by accident. For several months I had played around with an idea for my first solo title in a decade and a half, but it kept dancing away from me. Laying the idea aside to go off and write a collaborative book where my name appears after the word *with* didn't help. Although it sort of did. In my other writing life as a collaborator, I have had the privilege of working with a wide variety of people who have reshaped how I see myself and the world. This book would not exist without their influence.

As a collaborative writer, I assume the identities of those with whom I am writing. I like to say I crawl inside of their heads, but really, it is the other way around. They crawl into mine. We will spend hours upon hours together as I listen to their stories and ask probing questions. My goal is to see through their eyes and think like they think. For four to six months I literally have to lay myself aside and become another person for the eight or more hours a day I spend pecking away at my keyboard. With many, the dive into their identities goes so deep that I dream at night as the people with whom I work.

Inevitably, becoming other people changed me. Looking at the world through the eyes of an A-list actor as well as a missionary who spent two years in a North Korean prison changed my perspective. Through my collaborative career, I worked with families who endured unthinkable loss as well as with a young man who enlisted in the Marine Corps shortly after 9/11, only to come home two weeks after his first deployment missing both legs above the knees. I worked with multiple people who spent years in refugee camps on opposite sides of the world as well as with a man who grew up on the streets of Kampala, Uganda. You cannot spend the amount of time with each that I have and come away the same. I've worked with two paraplegics who somehow managed to walk again, and with the man who discovered CTE, the brain disease that kills football players. Every person with whom I have worked, from one of the most popular stars of ABC's *The Bachelor* to the number one real estate agent in the world to the unlikely best friends of an innocent man and the cop who put him in prison, has forced me to rethink my own assumptions about just about everything in this life. All of my collaborative work pushed me out of the happy little bubbles I often didn't even realize I was in. This book is the result, and I could not be happier about it.

So thank you to Andy Pettitte; Clay and Renee Crosse; Stephen Baldwin, who was the first person I fully became in my mind, which, if you know Stevie B, is a scary thought; Don and Susie Van Ryn; Newell and Collen Cerak; Whitney Cerak Wheeler; Alec Baldwin, who transformed my understanding of and relationship with my own father; Jerry Yang; Josh Bleill; Ed Thomas, who crawled in my head in such a powerful way even though I never had the privilege of meeting him because of the tragedy that prompted my writing his story; Lopez Lomong, who helped me mentally prepare to adopt my daughters from Africa; John Maclean, who was the first person I became in my dreams; Kenneth Bae; Ben Utecht; Bennet Omalu; Jamal McGee and Andrew Collins; Ainsley Earhardt; Cole and Savannah Labrant; Chris and Emily Norton; Lance Cooper, who opened my eyes to the full impact of the fall in Genesis 3; Kailen and Kyrah Edwards; Peter Mutabazi; and Jordan Cohen. Thanks to Jordan, if this writing thing doesn't work out, I can go sell real estate. He gave me all his secrets, even ones that didn't make it into our book. I also want to say a special word of thanks to Ben Higgins, because it was while working together that the original idea for this book started to form, in part from the many questions we bounced back and forth. Without the hours upon hours that I spent with all of you, I would not be the person I am today, and this book would not exist. I am forever grateful for each of you.

# ACKNOWLEDGMENTS

To Valerie, thank you for believing in me and taking this ride with me over the past forty-plus years. You only thought you married a firefighter back in 1982.

To my good friend and agent, Wes Yoder, thank you for your incredibly enthusiastic reception of this book every step of the way. You got it right away and encouraged me to keep pushing the envelope. I can't wait to do more subversive projects together.

To my editor at Revell, Rachel McRae, I cannot thank you enough for how you became the champion for this project at Revell and for your input through the writing process. I appreciate you more than you know. I also want to thank Kristin Kornoelje, Olivia Peitsch, Megan Draper, and everyone else at Revell/Baker Books who had a part in this book's journey.

To my oldest daughter and author in her own right, Bethany Mauger, thank you for being my sounding board as I wrote this book. Chapter 3 was your idea. Thank you as well to my daughters Hannah, Sarah, Meskerem, and Yeabsera for allowing me to tell stories about our life together. Being your dad has been my greatest privilege.

And finally, I want to thank my friends Scott, Laura, Mike, Teresa, Corey, Jennifer, Chase, Melany, Gary, and Lori for that evening in my living room, talking about God stuff when I blurted out the question that had been in my head for a while: "I wonder if I am a better Christian on Zoloft?" Your response and the discussion that followed turned what had been a foggy idea into a fully formed book.

A firefighter turned pastor turned writer and ghostwriter, award-winning author Mark Tabb has authored/coauthored over forty books, including the number one *New York Times* bestseller *Mistaken Identity*. Mark's books have been translated into many languages and published all over  the world. He lives in Indiana with his wife of forty-plus years and a tyrannical dachshund. Visit MarkTabb.com for more info.

## CONNECT WITH MARK:

🌐 MarkTabb.com

ⓕ @Mark.Tabb.355

◉ @Author_Mark_Tabb

ⓑ @Author_Mark_Tabb

✺ @AuthorMarkTabb

♪ Author.Mark.Tabb

Dear Reader,

Thank you for selecting a Revell book! We're so happy to be part of your life through this work.

Revell's mission is to publish books that offer hope and help for meeting life's challenges, and that bring comfort and inspiration. We know that the right words at the right time can make all the difference; it is our goal with every title to provide just the words you need.

We believe in building lasting relationships with readers, and we'd love to get to know you better. If you have any feedback, questions, or just want to chat about your experience reading this book, please email us directly at publisher@revellbooks.com. Your insights are incredibly important to us, and it would be our pleasure to hear how we can better serve you.

We look forward to hearing from you and having the chance to enhance your experience with Revell Books.

The Publishing Team at Revell Books
A Division of Baker Publishing Group
publisher@revellbooks.com